Travel Guide To San Sebastian 2023

Discover the Jewel of the Basque Coast: Exploring San Sebastian in 2023

Scott O. Cortes

Table Of Content

Museums and Art Galleries

INTRODUCTION

Thank you for visiting "Travel Guide to San Sebastian 2023: Discover the Jewel of the Basque Coast." We cordially encourage you to set out on a memorable adventure to one of Spain's most alluring locations using this thorough travel guide. San Sebastian is a city famed for its breathtaking scenery, extensive history, active culture, and top-notch cuisine. It is located along the magnificent Basque Coast.

Everyone may find something to enjoy in San Sebastian, regardless of their interests in food, beaches, outdoor activities, or culture. This book is intended to give you all the knowledge and advice you need to make the most of your trip to this alluring city in 2023.

You may immerse yourself in the history of the city and enjoy the flavours of Basque cuisine by following us as we lead you through the charming streets of the Old Town (Parte Vieja) in this guide. We will direct you to La Concha Beach and Zurriola Beach's magnificent sands, where you can soak up the sun or catch the ideal wave.

We will reveal the breathtaking hiking trails, scenic routes, and water sports activities that will enable you to experience San Sebastian's natural treasures if you are looking for outdoor adventures. We will also show you the bustling cultural scene, which includes everything from pelota games and traditional Basque festivals to a thriving art and music scene.

Additionally, this book will give you useful advice on organising your trip, such as the ideal times to go, lodging possibilities, and financial preparation ideas. To make your stay easy and pleasurable, we'll also provide advice on transportation, safety, and regional customs.

San Sebastian will leave a lasting impression on your emotions in addition to being a place to visit. Join us as we discover San Sebastian's hidden beauties, savour its gastronomic treats, and enjoy its distinct fusion of history and modernity.

In 2023, get ready to explore San Sebastian's beauty and mysteries as we set out on an unforgettable voyage. The journey has begun!

Welcome to San Sebastian

Thank you for visiting San Sebastian, the crown treasure of the Basque Coast. As soon as you set foot in this quaint city, you'll be enthralled by its singular combination of scenic beauty, cultural diversity, and culinary delights. San

Sebastian provides a gorgeous backdrop for a wonderful trip, nestled between the Bay of Biscay's azure waters and the region's undulating hills.

San Sebastian, also referred to as Donostia locally, has a long and illustrious history. It began as a modest fishing community and has since expanded into a vibrant city while maintaining its unique Basque identity. You'll find well-preserved houses, typical Basque architecture, and a warm, welcoming environment as you stroll through the Old Town's (Parte Vieja) winding lanes.

The renowned La Concha Beach, a crescent-shaped stretch of coastline encircled by beautiful green mountains, is one of the city's crowning beauties. You can unwind on the fine sand, go swimming in the clear water, or just take in the stunning views of the bay from here. Go to Zurriola Beach if you enjoy surfing there, you can catch some of the greatest waves in all of Europe.

With more Michelin stars per capita than any other city in the world, San Sebastian is known as a culinary haven. A variety of bite-sized Basque specialties are served at innumerable taverns and restaurants as part of the city's pintxos culture. As you indulge in the regional flavours and set out on a culinary journey, sample the delectable pintxos combined with the best Basque wines.

San Sebastian is a city of culture and innovation in addition to its gastronomic scene. Visit prominent museums that feature the works of well-known Basque artists, like the San Telmo Museum and the Chillida-Leku Museum, to fully immerse yourself in the thriving cultural scene. The city is bustling with events all year long, from the exuberant Semana Grande to the customary Basque dance and music celebrations.

San Sebastian has everything you might want, whether you're looking for outdoor adventures, cultural encounters, or just a peaceful getaway. As you travel through this fascinating city, take in the gorgeous scenery, enjoy wonderful cuisine, and bask in the warm hospitality of the locals.

Welcome to San Sebastian, where gastronomy, culture, and beauty join together to create an unforgettable vacation experience that you will remember for the rest of your life. Enjoy your vacation and allow San Sebastian's charms to charm you!

About this Guide

Your go-to travel companion for exploring and taking advantage of everything San Sebastian has to offer is "Travel Guide to San Sebastian 2023: Discover the Jewel of the Basque Coast". This thorough book has been painstakingly created to give you useful details, insider knowledge, and helpful suggestions to make your vacation to San Sebastian unforgettable.

You may find thorough explanations and suggestions for the city's main attractions inside this book, including must-see monuments, hidden jewels, and off-the-beaten-path locations. This book will meet all of your travel needs, whether you want to take in the local food, relax on the lovely beaches, go on outdoor excursions, or explore the Old Town.

This article provides information on the ideal time to visit San Sebastian so you can take advantage of pleasant weather and exciting festivals and successfully plan your vacation. Along with advice on spending and budgeting, it offers lodging choices to meet different needs and price ranges as well as helpful pointers for utilising the city's transit infrastructure.

As you read through the chapters, you'll discover in-depth details on San Sebastian's culinary scene, which is famed for its pintxos culture and Michelin-starred restaurants. Learn about traditional Basque cuisines, experience their flavours, and get suggestions for the best restaurants to try the regional specialties.

In addition, this book explores the city's rich cultural offerings, which range from attending exciting festivals to visiting museums and galleries that highlight the city's artistic legacy. Additionally, there are recommendations for outdoor pursuits that will let you take in the Basque Coast's breathtaking scenery, including hiking paths, surfing places, and beautiful drives.

This guide offers useful information on regional customs and etiquette, safety advice, emergency contacts, and necessary Basque phrases to ensure a smooth and pleasurable vacation. A list of suggested readings and internet sources is also provided to help you learn more about San Sebastian and the region around it.

This guide is intended to meet your requirements and interests, whether you're a frequent traveller or a first-time visitor, so you can get the most out of your time in San Sebastian. Make it your go-to guide for finding hidden gems, creating itineraries, and experiencing the diverse culture of this amazing city.

Prepare yourself for an extraordinary journey as you explore San Sebastian's history, take in its natural beauty, indulge in its delectable cuisine, and make lifelong memories. Let this manual be your dependable travel companion as you explore the Basque Coast in 2023.

Getting Around San Sebastian

San Sebastian provides a range of transportation choices to make it easy for you to go around the city and its surroundings. Here are the main ways to travel about San Sebastian, whether you like taking the bus or walking around on foot:

Walking: San Sebastian is a city that encourages pedestrians, and many of its attractions are close to one another. Enjoy a stroll through the Old Town's (Parte Vieja) picturesque streets, the promenades near the beaches, or the parks and gardens.

Public Buses: San Sebastian has a robust and interconnected public bus system. The buses travel through the suburbs, adjacent towns, and the city proper. Look for bus stops that have schedules and route maps posted. Tickets can be bought at kiosks or onboard the ship. When boarding, make sure you authenticate your ticket.

Regional train service known as Euskotren connects San Sebastian to various cities outside of the Basque Country. If you want to visit adjacent places like Zarautz or Hendaye (France), it's a practical choice. Examine the fares and schedules in advance.

Taxis: In the entire city, taxis are easily accessible. They are available for hailing on the street, at designated taxi stands, or through taxi app reservations. In San Sebastian, metre-based taxis may charge extra for carrying bags or overnight service.

DonostiaBizi, a bicycle-sharing program, is available in San Sebastian. Bicycles can be rented at several locations throughout the city. It's a wonderful way to tour San Sebastian's bike paths and take in the picturesque seaside pathways. Review the rental terms and conditions.

Car Rental: If having your car gives you more freedom, San Sebastian offers car rental services. But bear in mind that parking can be difficult, particularly in the city centre. For city exploration, it's best to park in designated spaces and take the bus or train.

Take the Pintxo Train for a fascinating and fun experience. You go by themed tourist train through the best pintxos establishments in the city on a culinary adventure. Enjoy the flavours while you relax and let the train take you to some of the top pintxos locations.

Consider the length of your stay, the destinations you want to see, and the form of transportation that best meets your needs and budget when organising your trip around San Sebastian. Make use of maps, guidebooks, and local resources to become familiar with the layout of the city and the locations of the public transit systems.

Always remember to check for any temporary schedule adjustments or holiday or special event alterations to transportation services. You can make the most of your time in San Sebastian and simply discover all the amazing sights and experiences the city has to offer by using the right mode of transportation.

Useful Travel Tips

Best Time to Visit: Because San Sebastian has a warm oceanic climate, you may go to any time of year. The busiest time of year is from June through August when the weather is good enough for beach activities.

The months of April to May and September to October are ideal for seeing the city because they provide milder temperatures and fewer tourists. The low season, from December to February, features lower temperatures and fewer visitors.

Accept the pintxos gastronomic heritage as part of your culture. In San Sebastian, you must try these little nibbles. Visit various pintxos bars and stroll the Old Town's winding lanes to savour a range of flavours. Keep in mind that it's normal to eat at the bar while standing up and to throw away your toothpicks and napkins on the floor.

Beach etiquette: Popular San Sebastian beaches like La Concha and Zurriola can grow congested during the summer months. Respect the swimming areas that have been specified, and heed any safety advice. While visiting the beach, be aware of your possessions and don't leave anything precious unattended.

Customs of the Area: The Basques are proud of their distinctive culture and language. Use the native greetings of "Kaixo" (hello) and "Agur" (goodbye) to respect the traditions of the area. Be considerate of others while observing the traditions and practices of the Basques. If you receive good service or support, don't forget to say "Eskerrik asko" (thank you).

Keep in mind that some stores and enterprises might have an afternoon siesta (break) between 2:00 PM and 5:00 PM. Some smaller shops and services can be momentarily shuttered at this time. Make appropriate plans for your shopping and activities.

Water from the tap is of a high standard in San Sebastian, so feel free to do so. It's an economical and environmentally good method to remain hydrated while you're there. Bring a refillable water bottle that you can use all day.

Language: The Basque language (Euskara) is frequently used as well as Spanish. Both languages may be used for announcements and signs. While knowing a few basic Spanish phrases can be useful, don't be afraid to ask locals whether they speak English or if they can help you.

San Sebastian organises several festivals and events throughout the year. The San Sebastian International Film Festival and Semana Grande (Big Week), two well-known events, are listed on the calendar. Accept the festive mood and take pleasure in the cultural activities and performances.

San Sebastian is a reasonably safe city, however, it's always advisable to exercise common sense caution. In busy places, keep an eye on your possessions and avoid exposing expensive goods to view. Utilise trustworthy transportation, and pay close attention to your surroundings, especially at night.

Even if San Sebastian has a lot to offer in terms of attractions, think about travelling outside the city. Visit adjacent cities like Bilbao, and Biarritz, or the picturesque seaside towns along the Basque Coast on day trips. These outings offer an opportunity to encounter the wider Basque culture and discover different topographies.

You'll be ready to enjoy your trip to San Sebastian by bearing in mind this practical travel advice. Enjoy your stay in this alluring city and savour the mouthwatering cuisine, breathtaking scenery, and rich culture it has to offer.

SAN SEBASTIAN AT A GLANCE

The beautiful coastal city of San Sebastian, commonly known as Donostia in Basque, is situated in northern Spain's Basque Country.

Travellers from all over the world now flock to San Sebastian because of its spectacular scenery, rich culture, and delectable gastronomy. Here is a little overview of what to expect when you travel to this wonderful city:

- Beautiful scenery can be found everywhere in San Sebastian, which is tucked between the Bay of Biscay and the gently sloping Basque countryside. There are three stunning beaches in the city, with the well-known La Concha Beach being a favourite among both locals and tourists. A picture-perfect scene is created by the golden sand, clean waterways, and backdrop of green mountains.

- San Sebastian is frequently praised as the culinary heaven and ideal vacation spot for foodies. Numerous Michelin-starred eateries can be found in the city, serving delectable Basque cuisine that fuses traditional flavours with cutting-edge cooking methods. Don't pass up the chance to sample pintxos, the well-known Basque equivalent of tapas, which can be found in the hopping taverns of the Old Town.

- **Cultural legacy:** San Sebastian has a diverse cultural legacy that blends modern influences with Basque customs. Discover the picturesque squares, ancient Old Town (Parte Vieja), and stunningly conserved architecture. The city also plays host to several cultural celebrations and events throughout the year, such as the vivacious Semana Grande, which includes dancing, music, and fireworks.

- **Art and Architecture:** San Sebastian is home to some spectacular structures, from opulent Belle Époque mansions to exquisite modernist structures. Visit Rafael Moneo's renowned Kursaal Congress Center and Auditorium or the Miramar Palace with its mesmerising bay vistas. Several top-notch museums, like the San Telmo Museum, which is devoted to Basque culture and history, are also located in the city.

- **Outdoor Activities:** San Sebastian offers a wide range of outdoor activities for nature lovers and adventure seekers. Mount Urgull or Mount Igueldo hikes offer sweeping vistas of the city and the sea. Explore the surrounding region to find lovely villages, verdant valleys, and scenic hiking paths.

- San Sebastian is firmly steeped in Basque culture and acts as a starting point for exploring the distinctive Basque character. Along with Spanish, the Basque language, Euskara, is widely spoken, and the people there are proud of their history and traditions. Participate in cultural activities, try out some traditional dances, or even visit rural Basque settlements to embrace the Basque spirit.

- San Sebastian is a place that truly enthrals the senses due to its blend of stunning natural scenery, world-class cuisine, and cultural diversity. San Sebastian offers a wide range of activities, including beach leisure, culinary exploration, outdoor exploration, and cultural immersion. This unique city on the Basque Coast will amaze you.

Brief History of San Sebastian

The history of San Sebastian is lengthy, fascinating, and rich. Here is a synopsis of its historical development:

- **Early Settlement:** People have lived in the region where San Sebastian is located since the Palaeolithic era. Roman ruins and ancient villages are both confirmed by archeological findings in the area.

- **Mediaeval Period:** In the 12th century, a fortified village was built on the hill of Urgull to ward off invaders, and this is when San Sebastian started to take shape as a settlement. The Church of San Sebastian served as the focal point for the village's growth and development, giving origin to its name.

- **Marine Importance:** During the Middle Ages, San Sebastian developed into a prominent port thanks to its advantageous coastline location, promoting trade and marine activity. The city's expansion was spurred by trade with surrounding areas and foreign countries.

- San Sebastian enjoyed favour with the Spanish monarchy in the sixteenth century. The city was given the honorific title of "Noble and Loyal" by Queen Isabella I of Castile in appreciation for its assistance during the conquest of Granada. Economic success and an increased reputation for the city were brought about by royal sponsorship.

- **Cultural Renaissance**: San Sebastian saw a period of cultural and architectural expansion during the 19th century. The elite and nobility of Europe began to flock to the city, where they constructed opulent houses and palaces along the scenic shoreline. San Sebastian had a reputation as a sophisticated and attractive beach resort throughout this period of growth.

- The calm existence of San Sebastian was disturbed by wars and political instability during the 20th century. The city was present during the terrible Spanish Civil War in the 1930s, which left its social structure and environment scarred. Despite this, it was able to rebuild and recover after the war.

- **Modern Period:** San Sebastian has seen a rebirth as a popular cultural, culinary, and tourism destination in recent years. The famed San Sebastian International

Film Festival in the city draws well-known directors and cinema buffs from all over the world. With its Michelin-starred restaurants and vibrant pintxos culture, San Sebastian's culinary industry has attracted attention from around the world.

San Sebastian has seen changes throughout its history, evolving from a sleepy fishing village to a busy port before becoming a popular tourist attraction. Today, it proudly displays its rich architectural legacy, breathtaking natural beauty, and thriving cultural scene, encouraging tourists to savour its enthralling past and allure.

Geography and Climate

On the eastern edge of the Bay of Biscay is San Sebastian, a city in northern Spain's Basque Country. It offers a distinctive combination of coastal and alpine terrain and is surrounded by beautiful natural scenery. An overview of San Sebastian's topography and climate can be found here:

- Geographically, San Sebastian is tucked between the sea and the lush hills of rural Spain. The Old Town (Parte Vieja), which serves as the city's historical core, is one of the city's several districts. One of the most recognizable sights in the city is La Concha Bay, with its crescent-shaped beach.

The surfers-favoured Zurriola Beach is located to the east of the bay. Beautiful scenery and natural features may be seen on Mount Urgull and Mount Igueldo, and the

Urumea River flows through the city.

- **Climate**: The Bay of Biscay and the Atlantic Ocean both have a modest oceanic influence on San Sebastian's weather. Moderate temperatures, copious rainfall, and a comparatively high humidity level define the climate.

Here are some of San Sebastian's climate's main characteristics:

- Summers in San Sebastian are warm and comfortable (June to August). The typical daytime temperature is between 20°C and 25°C (68°F and 77°F). However, sporadic heat waves have the power to raise temperatures. It is a great period for outdoor festivals and beach activities.

- **Winters in San Sebastian (December to February):** Daytime highs in San Sebastian during the winter months typically range from 8°C to 14°C (46°F to 57°F). Although it might be damp and rainy during this time of year, snowfall is uncommon. In San Sebastian, winter is regarded as the off-season for travellers.

- **Autumn (September to November) and Spring (March to May):** These seasons bring warm temperatures and are often excellent for outdoor activities. The range of daytime temperatures is 12°C to 18°C (54°F to 64°F). These times of year might be excellent for discovering the city and taking in San Sebastian's scenic surroundings.

- **Rainfall**: San Sebastian experiences high annual

precipitation. While the summer months get relatively less rain, October and November are the wettest months. It's a good idea to have a raincoat or umbrella with you, especially during the rainier months.

- Outdoor activities in San Sebastian, including strolling along the beaches and coastal promenades or going on a hike in the adjacent hills, have a magnificent backdrop thanks to the city's location and environment.

San Sebastian's natural beauty and temperate climate make it a pleasant destination year-round, whether you go in the hot summer months or the slower seasons.

Cultural Significance

San Sebastian is a significant cultural landmark both in the Basque Country and beyond the world. The city is well known for its thriving cultural scene, extensive history, and accomplishments in a variety of sectors. Here are some significant cultural features of San Sebastian:

- San Sebastian is regarded as a centre for Basque culture and traditions. The Basque people take great pleasure in their unique culture, language (Euskara), traditions, and history. The city acts as a starting point for discovering and comprehending Basque customs, music, dancing, and cuisine.

- San Sebastian's cuisine and gastronomy are highly regarded on a global scale. No other city in the world has more Michelin-starred eateries per resident than this one. Modern cuisine has been greatly shaped by its creative chefs and food artisans. With its distinctive approach to small, tasty nibbles, the pintxos culture has come to represent the culinary scene in San Sebastian.

- One of the oldest and most important film festivals in the world is the San Sebastian International Film Festival, which takes place every September. It was founded in 1953, features a variety of foreign films, and draws eminent directors, performers, and members of the film business. The festival showcases the city's ties to the film industry and enhances its cultural standing.

- San Sebastian is renowned for its beautiful architecture and thoughtful urban design. A fascinating fusion of architectural forms may be seen in the city's enormous Belle Époque structures, exquisite promenades, and well-preserved historical district. The city's architectural significance is aided by landmarks like the Rafael Moneo-designed Kursaal Congress Center and Auditorium.

- **Festivals and Cultural Events:** Throughout the year, San Sebastian hosts several festivals and cultural events to highlight its vivacious spirit and cultural diversity.

The city's Semana Grande event lasts a whole week in August and includes fireworks, street plays, concerts, and traditional Basque sports. Other occasions offer tourists an in-depth look at local culture by celebrating music, dance, theatre, and folklore.

- **Art and Museums:** There are numerous art museums and galleries in San Sebastian that provide insights into both modern and traditional Basque art. The Chillida-Leku Museum exhibits the creations of renowned Basque artist Eduardo Chillida, while the San Telmo Museum explores Basque culture and history. The relevance of the city's arts community is enhanced by these cultural institutions.

- **Sporting Events**: Cycling and surfing are two activities with a particularly significant presence in San Sebastian. The city has played host to international surfing contests as well as Tour de France leg stops. These sporting events attract athletes and sports fans from all over the world, further increasing the city's status as a cultural and sporting centre.

San Sebastian's deep-rooted Basque tradition, artistic accomplishments, gastronomic prowess, and capacity to host prestigious cultural events all contribute to the city's cultural relevance. It is a cultural gem on the Basque Coast and an alluring location for cultural study and enrichment due to its distinctive fusion of traditions, creativity, and natural beauty.

PLANNING YOUR TRIP

A seamless and enjoyable journey can be guaranteed with proper planning. Visiting San Sebastian is a thrilling adventure. Here are some crucial pointers to consider as you prepare to visit this wonderful city:

- **Choose the Best Time to Visit:** When deciding when to travel, take into account the seasons and your favourite activities. Spring (April to May) and autumn (September to October) both offer warmer temperatures and less crowded beaches, while summer (June to August) brings sunny weather and a thriving beach scene.

  The low season, from December through February, features colder temperatures but fewer visitors.

- Determine the number of days you intend to stay in San Sebastian. Think about how big the city is and how many things you want to do. Even while you can see the main sights in a few days, arranging for a longer stay will offer you more time to acquaint yourself with the culture, sample the cuisine, and go on day trips to neighbouring places.

- San Sebastian offers a variety of lodging choices to fit different needs and preferences. Due to its central location and bustling ambiance, the city core, especially the Old Town (Parte Vieja), is a favourite destination for travellers. If possible, reserve your lodging in advance, especially during festivals and high-demand times.

- Planning your travel to and within San Sebastian is advised. Public transit, such as buses and railways, has excellent connections across the city. San Sebastian Airport (EAS) is the closest airport for air travel, though you might alternatively think about flying into Bilbao Airport (BIO) or Biarritz Airport (BIQ) and then taking a transfer to San Sebastian.

You may easily explore the city on foot, but you can also take public transportation like buses or taxis.

- Make a list of the San Sebastian attractions that are a must-see based on your research. La Concha Beach, the Old Town with its winding alleyways and pintxos bars, Mount Urgull with its expansive vistas, and the Kursaal Congress Center are a few famous locations. The San Telmo Museum and the Naval Museum are just two of the top museums in San Sebastian.

- **Food and Dining:** The local cuisine is delectable, and San Sebastian is known for its gastronomy. Discover the Old Town's pintxos bars and sample a selection of tiny dishes matched with regional beverages like Txakoli or Basque cider.

If you want to enjoy gourmet dining in San Sebastian, think about making appointments at Michelin-starred establishments far in advance.

- **Day travels:** San Sebastian makes a fantastic starting point for day travels to adjacent places. Consider travelling to Biarritz, a chic seaside resort across the French border, or Bilbao to view the Guggenheim Museum and the lovely old town. You can also tour the lovely Basque countryside and visit the charming cities of Getaria and Hondarribia.

- Check the weather prediction for the dates of your trip and pack accordingly. The weather in San Sebastian is typically pleasant, but it's a good idea to pack clothing because it can change throughout the day. Bring along comfy walking shoes, swimsuits for trips to the beach, and a waterproof jacket or umbrella in case it rains occasionally in the city.

- **Local Etiquette:** Become familiar with the customs and etiquette of the area. The environment in San Sebastian is renowned for being cordial and respectful. In pintxos bars, respect the customs of the community and observe the noise regulations. To converse with locals and demonstrate your appreciation for the language, learn a few fundamental Spanish or Basque words.

Consider buying travel insurance to safeguard yourself against any unforeseen circumstances, such as trip cancellations, medical problems, etc.

Best Time to Visit

The ideal time to visit San Sebastian will depend on your tastes and the experiences you hope to have while there. To assist you in making a choice, the seasons are broken down as follows:

- **Summer (June to August):** San Sebastian experiences its busiest travel period in the summer. With typical temperatures between 20°C and 25°C (68°F and 77°F), the climate is warm and perfect for beach sports. Festivals and other events bring the city to life, and the beaches are crowded.

  However, it could be congested and lodging costs might be higher. Summer is an excellent season to visit if you don't mind the crowds and want to take advantage of the lively environment.

- Compared to summer, spring (April to May) and autumn (September to October) offer milder weather and less crowding. With an average temperature range of 12°C to 18°C (54°F to 64°F), it is comfortable for tourism and outdoor exploration.

If you prefer a more sedate ambiance and want to avoid the busiest travel times, these seasons are great. The appeal of the city is enhanced in particular by the blooming flowers and lush foliage of spring.

- **Winter (December to February):** San Sebastian experiences a low season during this time. It can be damp and rainy, with colder temperatures of 8°C to 14°C (46°F to 57°F). However, if you don't mind the lower temperatures and sporadic downpours, winter might provide a less expensive experience with fewer visitors. It's a fantastic opportunity to take in the local food, see the city's cultural attractions, and relax in a welcoming setting.

- A noteworthy event that brings in a sizable number of tourists and fosters a lively atmosphere is the San Sebastian International Film Festival, which takes place in September in San Sebastian. September might be a terrific time to go if you want to take in the festival or all the excitement that goes along with it.

Your personal preferences, tolerance for crowds, and the kind of experience you're looking for will ultimately determine the best time to visit San Sebastian.

Every season provides opportunities to explore the city's attractions, savour its culinary treats, and take in its cultural offerings as well as its special charm.

Duration of Stay

Depending on your interests, free time, and the activities you intend to perform, you can choose a different length of stay in San Sebastian.

While it is possible to see the main sights in a few days, planning for a longer stay will allow you to have a more immersive experience and truly enjoy the charm of the city. You can use the following factors to determine how long you will stay:

- **Sightseeing & Cultural Exploration**: A stay of two to three days would be adequate to view the main sights in San Sebastian, including La Concha Beach, the Old Town, Mount Urgull, and the San Telmo Museum. This amount of time will allow you to visit the city's attractions, savour the cuisine, and take in the ambiance.

- San Sebastian is well-known for its culinary culture, which includes pintxos bars and Michelin-starred restaurants. Consider extending your stay by 4 or 5 days if you're a foodie and want to experience all the city's culinary wonders.

  This will offer you plenty of time to try different pintxos, eat at other establishments, and even participate in a cooking class or food tour.

- **Beach and Outdoor Activities**: You might want to plan a longer trip if you want to take advantage of San Sebastian's beaches, water sports, and outdoor activities like swimming, hiking, or surfing. You can extend your trip by a few days to enjoy relaxing beach time, local coastline exploration, or day trips to the stunning Basque countryside.

- **Day Visits & Exploring the Neighborhood:** San Sebastian makes a fantastic starting point for day visits to adjacent places. Consider extending your stay by a few days to allow for excursions to attractive coastal towns or destinations outside of the city, such as Bilbao or Biarritz.

In conclusion, a minimum stay of 2 to 3 days will enable you to experience the highlights of San Sebastian. However, extending your stay to 4 to 7 days would be great if you want a more thorough experience that includes immersing yourself in the local culture, enjoying the cuisine, and visiting the surroundings. The length of your stay should ultimately be determined by your interests, free time, and the level of immersion you desire in this enchanting city.

Budgeting and Expenses

To ensure a pleasant and happy stay, it is crucial to take your budget into account while making travel plans to San Sebastian. When making travel plans on a budget, keep the following things in mind:

- San Sebastian has a variety of lodging choices, including inexpensive hostels, moderately priced hotels, and opulent resorts. The price of lodging will vary according to location, amenities, and the season of the year you visit.

  Budget-conscious tourists can find inexpensive lodging alternatives in the city, especially if they make reservations in advance or think about staying in nearby cities that are close to San Sebastian.

- **Meals and Dining**: Eating out is a highlight of any trip to San Sebastian because of its renowned culinary scene. Where you choose to eat can affect how much a meal costs. With pintxos typically costing between 1 and 3 euros each, the Old Town's pintxos bars provide a wide selection of cheap selections.

  Michelin-starred restaurants can be more pricey, with multi-course dinners costing anything from 100 to 300 euros per person. Choosing balanced meals and creating a daily food budget will help you keep costs under control.

- San Sebastian's public transportation system, which includes buses and railways, is effective. Buses are a practical and economical means of getting around the city. A single bus ticket typically costs 1.70 euros. Consider the cost of additional bus or train tickets if you intend to explore the neighbourhood or go on day trips. Although they are more expensive, there are taxis available.

- **Activities and Attractions**: Many of San Sebastian's attractions, including the beaches, public parks, and Old Town, are free or extremely inexpensive to enjoy. There may be admission charges for some museums and particular events, though. It's a good idea to do some research on the attractions you want to see and account for any charges.

- **Day Trips and Excursions:** Take into account the cost of transportation, admission fees, and any guided tours or activities if you intend to take day trips to nearby locations like Bilbao or

Biarritz. Budgeting for these extra experiences can be made easier by doing your research on costs and making plans in advance.

- **Shopping and souvenirs:** There are many places to shop in San Sebastian, including boutiques, marketplaces, and specialty shops. Set a spending limit for souvenirs and shopping while keeping in mind that some regional goods, such as Basque food or traditional crafts, may have higher price tags.

- **Miscellaneous Expenses**: It's wise to carry some additional cash or set aside money in case of emergencies, last-minute purchases, or other unplanned costs when travelling.

- When planning your travel budget, keep in mind to account for foreign exchange rates as well as any additional costs related to international transactions.

In general, the price of a trip to San Sebastian can change based on your travel preferences, length of stay, and travel style.

You can have a comprehensive grasp of your costs and guarantee a memorable and affordable trip to this lovely Basque city by budgeting, preparing ahead, and studying costs for lodging, meals, transportation, and activities.

Accommodation Options

The city of San Sebastian provides a variety of lodging options to fit various spending limits and tastes. Here are a few well-liked choices to think about:

- **Hotels**: San Sebastian features a range of hotels, from high-end hotels to more affordable ones. There are well-known global chains, quaint family-run hotels, and boutique hotels. Most hotels are found in the heart of the city, near tourist hotspots and the beach.

- **Guesthouses and Bed & Breakfasts:** These accommodations offer a cosier, more domestic feel. They frequently offer more individualised service and fewer accommodations. These lodgings can provide a relaxing stay with a dash of regional flair.

- Hostels are a terrific choice if you're travelling on a tight budget or desire a social setting. Numerous hostels in San Sebastian have inexpensive private rooms or dormitory-style accommodations.

  Additionally, some hostels plan social events and offer areas where visitors can socialise.

- **Apartments and vacation rentals**: For those looking for additional space and the freedom of self-catering, renting an apartment or vacation rental may be a viable option. You can select a place that meets your requirements from a variety of websites and organisations that offer a large selection of flats and holiday houses in San Sebastian.

- **Campgrounds:** The region around San Sebastian offers a few campgrounds for outdoor enthusiasts and people who are travelling with camping equipment. These campgrounds frequently provide amenities and services for tents, caravans, and RVs, allowing you to take advantage of the area's breathtaking scenery.

- Think about things like location, amenities, closeness to activities, and your budget when choosing your lodging. Due to its central location and lively ambiance, the city core, especially the sections near Old Town and La Concha Beach, is well-liked by tourists.

  However, other areas, including Gros and Antiguo, too provide a variety of lodging options and have a certain charm of their own.

- It's a good idea to reserve your lodging in advance, especially during busy times of the year or when the city is hosting important events. This will guarantee that you have more options and can get the finest prices.

When choosing a place to stay, keep in mind to read reviews, compare pricing, and take your trip's unique requirements into account..

EXPLORING SAN SEBASTIAN

Exploring San Sebastian provides a variety of activities, from thriving culinary scenes and cultural delights to gorgeous vistas and stunning architecture. When exploring the city, keep the following in mind:

- **Old Town (Parte Vieja):** Start your trip at San Sebastian's Old Town, the city's historic core. Explore the picturesque buildings, boutique stores, and pintxos bars that line its small lanes. Visit the gothic-style San Vicente Church and the bustling Constitution Square.

- La Concha Beach is a must-see destination and one of the most well-known urban beaches in all of Europe. Take a leisurely stroll down the promenade, swim in the clear waters, or just unwind on the sand and take in the beautiful scenery.

- Atop Mount Urgull, you may get a bird's-eye perspective of San Sebastian. Discover the Sagrado Corazón statue and the Castillo de la Mota, a stronghold from the 12th century, as you stroll through the park. Awe-inspiring views of the city and the Bay of La Concha are the hike's reward.

- **Kursaal Congress Center:** The Kursaal Congress Center is a spectacular example of contemporary architecture and a representation of San Sebastian's modern culture. If there is an event happening while you are there, admire its distinctive design and attend a concert or exhibition.

- Visit San Sebastian's museums to fully immerse yourself in the city's rich cultural legacy. The Naval Museum provides insights into the city's maritime traditions, while the San Telmo Museum exhibits Basque history and art.

The Victoria Eugenia Theatre, a legendary performing arts facility, and the Chillida-Leku Museum, a museum devoted to the sculptures of Eduardo Chillida, are two further noteworthy museums.

- Funicular rides up Monte Igueldo will give you sweeping views of San Sebastian and the surrounding area. Families or anyone looking for a nostalgic experience would love the amusement park at the top, which has vintage rides.

- **Basque Cuisine:** San Sebastian is known for its excellent cuisine, so make sure to try some of it. By visiting various pintxos bars and enjoying a variety of delectable snacks, you may learn about the distinctive tradition of pintxos (Basque tapas).

  Local delicacies like txakoli wine, bacalao (salted cod), and rich Basque cheesecake should not be missed.

- **Day trips:** San Sebastian is a great starting point for exploring the neighbourhood. Think about taking day trips to nearby places like Bilbao, which is home to the Guggenheim Museum, or Hondarribia, a quaint coastal town. You may also travel into the lovely Basque countryside to see charming villages like Getaria, which is well-known for its seafood and mediaeval appeal.

- **Festivals & Events**: Find out whether there are any festivals or events taking place while you are in San Sebastian. The city holds a number of well-known events throughout the year, including the San Sebastian International Film Festival, Jazzaldia, and Semana Grande with its vibrant celebrations and fireworks.

- San Sebastian provides opportunities for those who enjoy the great outdoors. Explore the city's bike-friendly paths by renting a bike, going for a hike along the coastal trails, or learning to surf at Zurriola Beach.

Keep in mind to take your time and appreciate San Sebastian's laid-back and pleasant atmosphere. Discovering the city's energetic streets, cultural landmarks, and scenic surroundings will definitely produce priceless memories.

Old Town (Parte Vieja)

In San Sebastian, Old Town, also known as Parte Vieja, is a fascinating district that presents a delicious fusion of history, culture, and gastronomic pleasures. What to expect when touring this wonderful region is as follows:

- **Streets and Architecture:** Explore the Old Town's winding streets and take in the distinctive architecture. Take in the colourful façade, wooden balconies, and elaborate ironwork of the well-preserved buildings. Every nook of the character-filled, winding streets offers a surprise just waiting to be found.

- Constitution Square (Plaza de la Constitución) is a great place to start your visit to the Old Town. This bustling plaza is surrounded by lovely structures and serves as a hub for both inhabitants and visitors. You can still make out the numbered balconies that were originally used to seat people during bullfights and other public events that were held there.

- **Churches and Religious Sites:** In the Old Town, stop by the beautiful Gothic-style church known as the San Vicente Church. Enter to experience its beautiful interior and serene environment. You can also visit other places of worship, such as the magnificent Baroque-style Basilica of Saint Mary of the Chorus.

- The Old Town is well known for its thriving food culture, especially its pintxos bars. These bars offer a selection of little, delectable pieces that are skewered on toothpicks and served on slices of bread. Participate in the local custom of "poteo," when you visit various bars, trying out different pintxos while sipping wine or a cool beverage. La Cuchara de San Telmo, Gandarias, and Bar Zeruko are a few of the area's well-known pintxos establishments.

- **Local Markets**: Visit the Old Town's local markets to take in the lively atmosphere and locate fresh produce, regional delicacies, and other goods. You may find a vast range of ingredients, such as fish, fruits, vegetables, and more, at the thriving Bretxa Market. It's a terrific place to get acquainted with the regional cuisine and maybe even pick up some supplies for a picnic or a home-cooked meal.

- **Plaza de la Trinidad**: Situated outside of the Old Town, Plaza de la Trinidad is a busy gathering place. It's a terrific spot to unwind, enjoy a drink, and take in the bustling environment because it is surrounded by bars and restaurants with outside seating. Live music shows and other cultural events are frequently held in the area, which fosters a lively atmosphere.

- **Cultural Sites:** The Old Town is home to cultural sites that are interesting to explore in addition to its culinary delights. Visit the San Telmo Museum to see Basque history, culture, and art. It is close to Constitution Square.

  It is housed in a former Dominican convent and features interesting exhibits that provide light on the area's history. The San Telmo Museum is also nearby, and it is located in a gorgeous old building.

Take your time as you stroll around the Old Town to discover the secret passageways, take in the vibrant ambiance, and savour the gastronomic treats that make this area a highlight of any trip to San Sebastian.

La Concha Beach

One of San Sebastian's most recognizable and gorgeous urban beaches, La Concha Beach is famous for its breathtaking beauty and energetic environment. What to anticipate when visiting La Concha Beach is as follows:

- La Concha Beach is located in a lovely bay that is bordered by Mount Urgull and Mount Igueldo. The beach has a crescent shape, smooth golden sand, and blue water that is extremely clean. A picture-perfect scene is created by the magnificent hills in the background and the adorable island of Santa Clara in the distance.

- Wide promenades are positioned along the beach, providing a pleasant stroll along the water's edge. Enjoy a leisurely stroll while taking in the stunning views of the bay and the sunshine. Additionally, the promenade is lined with benches that are ideal for relaxing while taking in the view.

- **Swimming and relaxation:** La Concha Beach is a great place for both. During the hot summer months, the tranquil waters provide a cool respite and are safe for swimming. You may enhance your beach experience and discover the ideal area to unwind by renting sun loungers and umbrellas.

- **Water Sports:** La Concha Beach provides a variety of water sports activities if you're looking for some adventure. Rent a kayak, a paddleboard, or even attempt wave surfing. Along the beach, there are a number of water sports facilities that rent out equipment and provide starting instruction.

- **Miramar Palace**: The magnificent Miramar Palace is located at the eastern end of La Concha Beach. The Spanish royal family erected this opulent palace in the 19th century as a getaway. Today, it functions as a cultural hub and, from its surrounding gardens, provides breathtaking views of the beach and the bay.

- La Concha Beach serves as a location for a number of events and festivals throughout the year. In addition to hosting the International Triathlon in the summer, it serves as the starting point for the well-known "Cavalcade of Magi" parade during the Christmas season. During your visit, keep an eye out for any special events.

- **Beachside Cafés and Restaurants**: There are a number of beachside cafés and restaurants along La Concha Beach's promenade where you can have a delicious meal or a cool drink while taking in the scenery. Enjoy delectable Basque food, unwind on a terrace, and take in the seaside environment.

- **Santa Clara Island:** The lovely Santa Clara Island is located off the shore of La Concha Beach. A short boat journey will get you to the island, where you may spend a few hours exploring its rocky coastlines, hiking its paths, or just taking in the peace and quiet of this natural haven.

La Concha Beach provides a lovely and welcoming setting whether you're wanting to sunbathe, swim, go for a stroll with your significant other, or engage in water sports. Both locals and tourists adore it because of its beauty and energetic vibe.

Monte Urgull

In the centre of San Sebastian, on the Monte Urgull hill, there are magnificent views of the city, the coast, and the Bay of La Concha. What to anticipate when visiting Monte Urgull is as follows:

- **Panoramic Views**: The stunning panoramic views of San Sebastian and its surrounds are a reward for climbing Monte Urgull. You can enjoy expansive views of the city's roofs, the bay's glistening waters, the charming La Concha Beach, and the far-off mountains from the peak.

  It's the perfect location for shooting priceless photos and enjoying the area's natural splendour.

- Monte Urgull has a long history, which is important today. The Castillo de la Mota, a castle built in the 12th century, is located at the peak. Discover the military past of the area by exploring the castle's walls, cannons, and exhibitions. Additionally, you may go to the Sagrado Corazón statue, a monumental sculpture that serves as San Sebastian's emblem.

- **Walking Trails:** Monte Urgull has a number of walking paths that weave through its verdant landscape and provide a tranquil respite from the bustle of the city.

You'll discover delightful hidden nooks, tiny gardens, and overlooks that offer various perspectives of San Sebastian as you explore the hill. All fitness levels can use the trails because of their varied levels of difficulty and excellent maintenance.

- **Historical Monuments:** In addition to the castle and the Sagrado Corazón statue, Monte Urgull is home to a number of other historical structures.

  The Monument to the Sacred Heart of Jesus, a statue honouring the victims of the Spanish Civil War, and the English Cemetery, a burial ground for British soldiers who fought in the Peninsular War, are two examples.

- **Nature and wildlife**: A wide variety of flora and fauna can be found in Monte Urgull. You might run into squirrels, birds, and other tiny animals as you explore the hill. It is the perfect location for nature lovers and those looking for a peaceful break from the city because of the vegetation and peaceful ambiance.

- Visit the Interpretation Center on Monte Urgull to discover more about the history, vegetation, and fauna of the hill as well as the cultural importance of San Sebastian. The centre provides a broader understanding of the area through educational displays, exhibits, and interactive presentations.

- **Events & Festivals:** Monte Urgull is used as a location for a number of cultural events and festivals throughout the year. Watch out for any events like concerts, plays, and other performances that can occur on the hill, offering a distinctive approach to take in San Sebastian's thriving artistic and cultural environment.

- **Exercise and recreation**: Monte Urgull is a popular location for both locals and tourists to engage in physical activity and leisure pursuits. Along the trails, you can jog or take a leisurely stroll while taking in the fresh air and stunning surroundings. It's a well-liked destination for nature lovers and a fantastic way to be active while you're there.

To get the most out of your visit to Monte Urgull, dress comfortably for walking, bring water, and think about going when it's cooler out. Exploring this historic hill offers a fascinating fusion of history, nature, and stunning vistas, as well as a distinctive viewpoint on San Sebastian.

Monte Igueldo

San Sebastian's Monte Igueldo is a charming hill that provides stunning panoramic views over the city, the Bay of La Concha, and the nearby shoreline. What to anticipate when visiting Monte Igueldo is as follows:

- **Funicular journey**: Take a pleasant journey on the vintage funicular, which has been in service since 1912, to reach the summit of Monte Igueldo. As it climbs the hill and gives picturesque vistas along the route, the funicular provides a delightful and nostalgic experience.

- **Panoramic Views:** From Monte Igueldo's summit, you'll have a stunning 360-degree panorama of San Sebastian. Enjoy the expansive views of the city's skyline, the crescent-shaped La Concha Beach, the bay's glistening waters, and the verdant surroundings. The summit's vantage point offers a wonderful opportunity for breathtaking photos and an unforgettable experience.

- **Amusement Park:** A vintage amusement park with a charmingly nostalgic aura may be found near the top of Monte Igueldo. The theme park has traditional rides like a Ferris wheel and a vintage roller coaster from 1928. Take in the excitement of the rides, discover the arcade, and savour classic fairground foods like cotton candy and popcorn.

- **Gardens & Picnic spots**: Monte Igueldo has lovely gardens and picnic spots, making it the perfect place to unwind and take in the tranquil ambiance. Enjoy the natural beauty of the area by taking a leisurely stroll through the groomed gardens, setting up a picnic in a shady area, or just relaxing on a bench.

- **Lighthouse**: The Faro de la Plata is a charming lighthouse that may be found on Monte Igueldo. This lovely lighthouse, which dates to the nineteenth century, contributes to the hill's picturesque appeal. Take a stroll to the lighthouse and take in the scenery there.

- **Trails for hiking and environment exploration:** Monte Igueldo has a number of trails for hiking and nature exploration that let you explore the hill's natural splendour and find secret treasures en route. Explore the area's rich vegetation, get up close to the wildlife and fauna, and take in the peace and quiet. Both leisurely walkers and ardent hikers can use the paths because they are designed to accommodate varied fitness levels.

- **Views of the sunset**: Monte Igueldo is a well-known location for admiring magnificent sunsets above San Sebastian. A magnificent atmosphere is produced when the sun descends below the horizon and the sky is painted in shades of orange, pink, and purple. Embrace the magnificence of this natural phenomenon by capturing the breathtaking sunset vistas.

- **Cafés and Refreshment Stands**: At Monte Igueldo's summit, you can find cafés and refreshment stands where you may get a snack, a cold beverage, or an ice cream cone. Take a rest, indulge in the regional cuisine, and take in the scenery.

A wonderful way to get away from the city, embrace nature, experience exhilarating rides, and take in breathtaking vistas is to visit Monte Igueldo. It is a must-see location in San Sebastian if you want to experience panoramic views and vintage amusement park thrills.

Zurriola Beach

In San Sebastian, there is a lively and dynamic beach called Zurriola Beach, also called Playa de Zurriola. Zurriola Beach, which is on the city's eastern edge and has a distinctive ambience, draws both locals and tourists. What to anticipate when visiting Zurriola Beach is as follows:

- Zurriola Beach is a well-known surfing location in San Sebastian. It draws surfers of all abilities because of its reliable waves and ideal weather. One of the surf schools nearby will teach you how to surf if you're a novice. The beach presents a thrilling opportunity for expert surfers to catch waves and feel the sport's exhilaration.

- **Surfing events:** Zurriola Beach hosts surfing events all year long that draw both domestic and foreign competitors. If you manage to go when one of these competitions is taking place, you'll see some great surfing performances and a buzzing environment as fans assemble to support the athletes.

- **Water Sports:** Zurriola Beach offers a range of other water sports in addition to surfing. Activities including bodyboarding, kayaking, and paddleboarding are available. Along the beach, equipment rental services are offered, making it simple for you to partake in these aquatic experiences.

- **Promenade along the beach:** Zurriola Beach is bordered by a roomy promenade that makes a lovely space for cycling, running, and strolling. Beautiful views of the beach and the Bay of La Concha can be found from the promenade. You may take a leisurely stroll along the waterfront while taking in the bustling ambiance and sea wind.

- **Chill-out Bars and Cafés:** There are several chill-out bars and cafés where you can unwind and enjoy the beachy atmosphere along the promenade and in the neighbourhood. These places provide a relaxed ambiance that is ideal for having a drink, getting a bite to eat, or just relaxing and taking in the landscape.

- **Beach volleyball:** Zurriola Beach has areas set aside for the sport, drawing both recreational players and tournaments. You can participate in a friendly match or watch the players demonstrate their abilities if you'd want to see some exciting beach volleyball action.

- **Outdoor Exercise:** There is plenty of space for outdoor exercise on the promenade and at the beach. Along the promenade, you'll find fitness stations and equipment that let you work out while taking in the coastal environment. It's an excellent location for bodyweight workouts, yoga, and jogging.

- **Views of the sunset:** Zurriola Beach provides a beautiful backdrop to take in the magnificent sunsets across the Bay of La Concha. The sky turns into a canvas of vivid colours as the sun sets, creating a wonderful atmosphere. Find a cosy area on the sand, relax, and take in the breathtaking sunset views.

- A bustling environment, tranquil coastal promenade, and the exhilaration of water sports are all present at Zurriola Beach. Whether you're an energetic beachgoer or just trying to relax, Zurriola Beach in San Sebastian offers a fun and exciting experience.

Paseo Nuevo

San Sebastian's Paseo Nuevo is a beautiful waterfront promenade that provides breathtaking views of the Bay of La Concha and the city's shoreline. What to anticipate when visiting Paseo Nuevo is as follows:

- **Coastline Views**: Paseo Nuevo offers a charming vantage point to take in San Sebastian's stunning coastline vistas. You may enjoy expansive views of the bay, the well-known La Concha Beach, and the surrounding cliffs as you stroll down the promenade. The expansive views may be enjoyed from Paseo Nuevo and make for amazing photo opportunities.

- **Seafront Walk:** Paseo Nuevo provides a pleasant and leisurely stroll alongside the water. The promenade, which goes along the cliffs and is well-maintained, enables you to take in the tranquillity of the surroundings and the reviving sea wind. The walk is popular with both locals and tourists because it is appropriate for people of all ages and fitness levels.

- **Sculptures and art:** The Paseo Nuevo is lined with sculptures and art installations that give the promenade a creative edge. As you explore the region, these artistic additions add to the lively environment and offer extra areas of interest.

- **Mirador de la Brecha**: The Mirador de la Brecha is a lookout that provides great panoramic views of the city and the bay, and it is situated along Paseo Nuevo. From this vantage point, you may view San Sebastian's splendour from a different angle and take beautiful pictures of the surrounding area.

- **Outdoor Cafés and Restaurants:** Paseo Nuevo is dotted with quaint outdoor cafés and eateries, making it the perfect place to have a leisurely meal or a cool drink while taking in the scenery. You may unwind at one of the places, eat delectable Basque food, and take in the ambience of the promenade and the sea.

- Paseo Nuevo is a well-known location to see breath-taking sunsets over the Bay of La Concha. The sky becomes alive with vivid colours as the sun sets beyond the horizon, creating a mystical and enchanting ambiance. The time is ideal for finding a cosy position along the promenade and admiring the sunset.

- **Access to Old Town:** The city's shoreline and the famed Old Town (Parte Vieja) are connected by the Paseo Nuevo. You can easily access the Old Town's winding streets, charming plazas, and lively ambiance from the promenade. It's an ideal place to begin learning about the dynamic neighbourhood's rich history, culture, and cuisine.

- **Local Events and Performances:** Paseo Nuevo occasionally hosts neighbourhood gatherings, plays host to street musicians, and offers local events and performances. During your visit, keep an eye out for any events or cultural activities going along the promenade.

- The natural splendour of San Sebastian's shoreline can be admired in a mesmerising and tranquil environment thanks to Paseo Nuevo. The Paseo Nuevo offers a lovely experience for tourists of all interests, whether they are looking for a tranquil stroll, a spot to unwind and take in the vistas, or a starting point to explore the city.

Miramar Palace

On a hilltop near San Sebastian, Miramar Palace is a magnificent palace with views of the Bay of La Concha. It is known for its spectacular architecture, attractive surroundings, and historical significance. What to anticipate when visiting Miramar Palace is as follows:

- **Background information**: Miramar Palace was constructed in the late 19th century as a getaway for the Spanish royal family. Queen Maria Cristina, the reigning monarch of Spain at the time, ordered it. The palace has been associated with royalty for its entire existence and has seen important historical occurrences.

- Miramar Palace is a beautiful example of a well-balanced fusion of architectural styles, particularly influenced by the English and French styles of the time. Grand facades, graceful arches, complex detailing, and magnificently planted gardens are all part of the palace's design. Its magnificent architecture is a monument to the period's workmanship.

- Miramar Palace is surrounded by vast gardens and verdant foliage, which add to its appeal and foster a calm ambiance. The well-kept gardens provide tranquil strolls, shady pathways, and great places to unwind and take in the scenery. Wander through the gardens at your own pace and take in the assortment of plants, flowers, and trees.

- **Panoramic Views:** Miramar Palace offers breath-taking panoramic views of the Bay of La Concha, the cityscape, and the nearby shoreline due to its high location. You can marvel at the magnificent panoramas and take beautiful pictures of the natural splendour from specific vantage points on the palace grounds.

- The Miramar Palace is a significant cultural and historical site in San Sebastian. It is a significant symbol of the city's heritage because of its lengthy history and royal links. Over the years, the palace has served a variety of functions and housed important people and occasions, adding to its cultural value.

- Concerts, cultural events, and exhibitions are frequently held at Miramar Palace. The palace's adaptability as a location for creative and cultural expressions is demonstrated by these events. To experience the lively atmosphere of the palace during your stay, keep an eye out for any scheduled events.

- Access to the seaside and beautiful walking pathways are provided on the palace grounds, allowing you to explore the area and take in the coastal views. There are access places to the shoreline along the pathways, where you may meander and take in the beauty of the bay and perhaps even dip your toes in the ocean.

- **A Calm Retreat**: Miramar Palace offers a calm escape from the busy city hub. It has a calm atmosphere because of its hilltop location, which is surrounded by nature and offers magnificent views. It's the perfect place to get away from the throng, unwind, and take in San Sebastian's splendour.

Visits to Miramar Palace provide visitors a look into the city's regal past and the chance to take in both the architectural splendour and the surrounding landscape. Miramar Palace is a must-see location in San Sebastian whether you're interested in history, architecture, or are just looking for a quiet escape.

Aquarium Donostia

San Sebastian is home to Aquarium Donostia, usually referred to as the San Sebastian Aquarium, which is a well-liked tourist destination. It is an interesting and instructive experience for guests of all ages and is located along the shoreline. What to expect when you go to the Aquarium Donostia is as follows:

- Aquarium Donostia's marine life exhibits feature a wide variety of aquatic creatures from the Cantabrian Sea and beyond. View a variety of fish, sharks, rays, turtles, and other aquatic species by exploring the numerous exhibits. Through its exhibits, the aquarium hopes to raise public awareness of and commitment to protecting marine habitats.

- **Oceanarium**: The Oceanarium, a huge tank that offers an immersive experience, is the aquarium's focal point. Visit the tunnel that runs beneath the tank to see the underwater life that is swimming all around you and above you. It's a rare chance to get up close and personal with sharks, rays, and other large species.

- Interactive touch tanks are available at the aquarium so that guests may get up close and personal with some marine life. Under the guidance of trained personnel, have the opportunity to touch and learn about sea stars, sea urchins, and other fascinating organisms.

- **Educational Programs**: For both individuals and groups, the Aquarium Donostia offers educational programs and guided tours. Learn about marine biology, environmental protection, and the significance of maintaining marine ecosystems. These shows improve environmental consciousness while offering insightful information about the undersea world.

- **Temporary Exhibitions**: The aquarium hosts short-term displays that highlight particular species or topics. These exhibits offer a new perspective on the wonders of the water and a broader understanding of numerous marine issues. If there are any special exhibitions happening while you are there, check the schedule.

- **Interactive Displays**: The aquarium is filled with engaging interactive displays for guests of all ages. Discover fascinating information about marine life, put your knowledge to the test with quizzes, and take part in interactive games and activities to make learning enjoyable and engaging.

- **Terrace outside**: The Aquarium Donostia has a terrace outside with sweeping views of the bay. While drinking a drink or getting a snack from the on-site café, take a moment to relax and take in the natural beauty. The terrace offers a tranquil location to take in the seaside atmosphere and take in the waterfront scenery.

- **Gift Shop:** Be sure to stop by the aquarium's gift shop before you depart. Look through a selection of trinkets, books, toys, and eco-friendly goods with a marine theme. It's a fantastic place to find unusual presents or souvenirs to keep as a reminder of your trip to the aquarium.

Discovering the wonders of the undersea world is an educational and pleasurable experience made possible by the Aquarium Donostia. The aquarium offers an immersive and instructive voyage into the depths of the sea, whether you're a marine fanatic, a family seeking educational activities, or just inquisitive about marine life.

GASTRONOMY IN SAN SEBASTIAN

San Sebastian's cuisine is renowned around the world, making it a true gourmet feast. San Sebastian has gained its reputation as a food lover's dream thanks to its many Michelin-starred restaurants, pintxos pubs, and a strong emphasis on regional products. What to expect from San Sebastian's cuisine is as follows:

- Pintxos are little, bite-sized culinary delicacies that are often served on a slice of bread and held together with a toothpick. San Sebastian is well known for its pintxos.

  The city has plenty of pintxos bars, notably in the Old Town (Parte Vieja) region. Every pub has a different menu of pintxos, ranging from inventive and original combinations to more conventional selections like jamón ibérico and tortilla Espanola. A well-liked pastime that lets you try a range of cuisines and cooking techniques is "pintxos hopping."

- **Michelin-Starred Restaurants**: San Sebastian is a great gastronomic destination thanks to its impressive collection of Michelin-starred eateries. These places display the skills of renowned chefs who make delicious dishes utilising the best regional products. You can savour a memorable meal at any number of renowned restaurants, including Arzak, Akelarre, Mugaritz, and Martin Berasategui.

- San Sebastian is in the centre of the Basque Country, and Basque cuisine is a prominent part of the city's gastronomic scene. The focus on premium ingredients, simplicity, and adherence to traditional cooking methods define Basque cuisine. On the menus of nearby restaurants, you may anticipate seeing dishes like ganguro (spider crab), kokotxas (hake or cod cheeks), and bacalao al pil-pil (codfish in a garlic and olive oil sauce).

- **Fresh Seafood**: Given its proximity to the seaside, San Sebastian is well-known for its selection of fresh seafood. There are many delicious seafood meals available, such as grilled fish, seafood stews, and marmitako (basque fisherman's stew).

Visit the bustling La Bretxa market to see the day's catch and buy fresh fish for your culinary creations.

- **Txakoli Wine**: The Txakoli wine region, which includes San Sebastian, is renowned for producing the distinctive and energising white wine known as txakoli.

Your culinary explorations in the city will be delightfully accompanied by this wine, which goes well with pintxos and seafood. Don't pass up the chance to taste some txakoli and tour the nearby wineries in the countryside.

- **Farmers Markets:** There are many farmers markets in San Sebastian where you may discover a wide variety of local, fresh produce. The most well-known of them is the Mercado de la Bretxa, where you can immerse yourself in a lively environment full of vibrant fruits, vegetables, cheeses, and other local goods. It's a terrific opportunity to get to know the regional flavours and engage with local food culture to visit these markets.

- **Food Festivals:** San Sebastian has several food festivals all year long to honour diverse gastronomic pleasures. The Semana Grande, one of the most well-known festivities, includes a contest for the greatest pintxos in the city. To emphasise the tight connection between food and film, the International Film Festival of San Sebastian also has a section devoted to culinary cinema.

- San Sebastian's culture and identity are fundamentally shaped by its cuisine. You'll find an unrivalled culinary experience that honours the rich flavours and traditions of Spain whether you're eating pintxos, dining at a Michelin-starred establishment, or perusing the neighbourhood markets.

Introduction to Basque Food

A culinary tradition known for its robust flavours, premium ingredients, and deeply ingrained cultural significance is Basque cuisine.

The cuisine of the Basque Country, which stretches across parts of northern Spain and southwestern France, is known across the world for its distinctive cooking methods and mouth watering meals. An introduction to the fascinating world of Basque cuisine is provided below:

- **Foods from Local Sources:** The use of seasonal and locally derived foods is highly valued in Basque cuisine. The area provides an abundance of fresh fruit, fish, meats, and dairy products because of its varied topography, which includes both mountains and coastline. The inherent qualities of its components are celebrated in Basque cuisine, which uses everything from farm-fresh vegetables to exquisite meats and delectable shellfish.

- The renowned Basque little plates known as pintxos are a true culinary art form. Usually served on a slice of bread, these bite-sized treats are topped with a variety of toppings, including cheese, fish, cured meats, and veggies.

Locals and tourists alike assemble at pintxos bars to try a broad variety of flavours and textures, and pintxos are frequently enjoyed as a sociable and communal dining experience.

- **Grilled food:** The Basque Country is renowned for its proficiency with grilling methods. In Basque cuisine, grilled meats are highly prized, particularly the legendary Txuleta, a thick cut of cow steak. Both professional chefs and home cooks take great pleasure in their grilling abilities, employing local hardwoods to give the food a characteristic smoky flavour.

- **Seafood Specialties**: Basque cuisine features an outstanding variety of seafood specialties due to its proximity to the Bay of Biscay. The region's coastal wealth, which includes coveted seafood like spider crab and baby eels (angular) as well as fresh fish like hake, cod, and anchovies, is used in a range of mouthwatering recipes.

Basque seafood recipes are a great joy for seafood lovers, whether they are grilled, poached, or marinated.

- **Traditional Stews and Soups:** Hearty stews and soups are a staple of Basque cuisine, especially during the colder months. The Basque fisherman's stew, or marmitako, one of the most well-known recipes, combines tuna or other fish with potatoes, peppers, and onions in a delicious broth.

Other regional stews, such as piperade, which is cooked with peppers, tomatoes, and onions, and bacalao al pil-pil, which is codfish in a sauce of garlic and olive oil, highlight the powerful flavours of the area.

- Idiazabal Cheese is one of the most well-known cheeses in Basque cuisine, which is known for its outstanding cheeses. This semi-hard cheese is created from the milk of Latxa and Carranzana sheep and is matured to give it a distinctive smoky flavour. Idiazabal cheese is frequently consumed on its own, in various recipes, or combination with regional honey or quince paste.

- Basque cuisine is frequently served with a glass of Txakoli wine. The freshness and lightness of this Basque Country white wine make it the ideal pairing with pintxos and seafood meals. It is crisp and gently effervescent. To aerate and heighten its effervescence, txakoli wine is frequently served with flair.

- The emphasis on premium products, time-honoured methods, and powerful flavours in Basque cuisine has made it a highly sought-after gastronomic experience. Basque cuisine offers an unforgettable culinary adventure that honours the cultural legacy and culinary prowess of the Basque people, whether you're touring the hopping pintxos bars, enjoying grilled meats, or indulging in the region's marine specialties.

Pintxos: The Basque Tapas

Pintxos, or "Basque tapas," are small, tasty nibbles that are an essential component of Basque cuisine and a treasured social custom. They are the quintessential culinary jewels of the Basque Country. An examination of pintxos, their history, and what makes them so unique follows:

- **Culture of Pintxos:** In the Basque Country, pintxos are more than just small appetisers. They stand for a way of life. The custom of partaking in pintxos is strongly ingrained in local society and provides a venue for friends and family to get together, interact, and savour a variety of delectable flavours.

- Spanish tapas are similar to pintxos, yet pintxos have their unique qualities. The name "pintxo" (which means "spike" or "thorn" in Basque) comes from the fact that pintxos are often served on a slice of bread and fastened with a toothpick or skewer. In contrast, tapas don't always come with bread and can include a wider variety of foods.

- **Variety of Flavors**: The tremendous variety of pintxos is one of their most appealing features. The excellent selection of small dishes available at pintxos bars includes both traditional classics and creative mashups. There are many varieties available, including vegetarian pintxos with roasted peppers or local cheeses, seafood pintxos with anchovies or grilled prawns, meat-based pintxos with cured ham or roasted beef, and much more.

- Pintxos serve as a blank canvas for creative culinary expression. By experimenting with flavours, textures, and presentations, chefs and cooks showcase their abilities. Each pintxo can be a unique work of art that has been painstakingly made with consideration for balance, harmony, and detail. The creativeness and enthusiasm of Basque chefs are evident in the way they combine the ingredients, sauces, and garnishes.

- Ingredients that are in season and that are sourced locally are highly valued in Basque cuisine, and pintxos are no exception. Pintxos honour the flavours of the Basque Country by showcasing the best local produce as well as the freshest seafood from the neighbouring coast.

These delicious bites will likely contain items like cod, tuna,

Idiazabal cheese, peppers, mushrooms, and more.

- A common way to enjoy pintxos is to embark on a pintxos hopping excursion, or "trinitro" in Basque. The streets of cities like San Sebastian, Bilbao, and Pamplona are lined with pintxos bars. As you walk from one place to another, you can experience a range of flavours because each bar has its distinctive assortment.

  You may fully immerse yourself in the colourful gastronomic culture of the Basque Country through this entertaining and social experience.

- **The Basque Ritual:** There is a specific protocol to observe when consuming pintxos. You'll often find the pintxos displayed on the bar counter rather than selecting them from a menu. After your meal, the server will count the toothpicks or skewers to determine your bill, and you are welcome to help yourself to any that catch your eye.

- **Txakoli and wine:** Txakoli, a regional Basque wine, is frequently paired with pintxos. The tastes of pintxos complement this white wine's acidity and subtle fizz well, enriching the overall dining experience.

Pintxos combine creativity, history, and community to represent the very best of Basque cooking.

Traditional Basque Dishes

The rich and varied culinary heritage of Basque cuisine is well known, and it includes a wide range of traditional dishes that highlight the distinctive tastes and ingredients of the area. When discovering the lively cuisine culture of the Basque Country, you should sample some of these typical Basque dishes:

- Salted cod is cooked in a sauce consisting of olive oil, garlic, and pil-pil, an emulsion made of the oil and fish juices, in the traditional Basque meal known as bacon al Pil-Pil. As a consequence, a delicious and mildly spicy dish is created that brings out the cod's delicate texture.

- Marmitako is a robust fisherman's stew that developed in the Basque Country's coastal areas. A tasty and warming dish is often produced by combining fresh tuna or other fish, potatoes, onions, green peppers, tomatoes, and olive oil.

- Leeks, potatoes, carrots, and other in-season vegetables are used to make the classic Basque vegetable soup pousada. It is cooked for a while to soften the veggies, resulting in a rich and filling soup that is ideal for chilly days.

- **Txangurro a la Donostiarra**: This meal highlights the spider crab, one of the most treasured marine products in the Basque Country. The crab shell is stuffed with crab meat and a tasty mixture of onions, tomatoes, garlic, and white wine. The crab is then baked till golden and fragrant.

- **Chuletón de Buey (beef rib-eye steak):** Basque cuisine is renowned for its superb grilled meats, of which the chuletón de buy (beef rib-eye steak) is a great example. This large, juicy steak is prepared over an open flame, frequently using hardwood charcoal, to produce a smoky, charred exterior and a juicy, tender interior.

- **Piperrada:** Made with sautéed bell peppers, onions, and tomatoes, piperrada is a typical Basque cuisine. The result is a colourful and savoury side dish or addition to other dishes that are frequently spiced with ingredients like paprika and occasionally include scrambled eggs or tuna.

- Gâteau Basque is a classic Basque dessert made of a buttery, flaky pastry filled with custard or a flavorful, fragrant cherry or almond filling. It is frequently served after a meal or with a cup of coffee as a sweet treat.

- Idiazabal Cheese is a well-known Basque cheese prepared from unpasteurized sheep milk. It has a characteristic smokey flavour that comes from the old-fashioned smoking method. This semi-hard cheese can be eaten on its own, drizzled with regional honey, or added to a variety of recipes and pintxos.

- **Tarta de Santiago**: Tarta de Santiago is a well-known dessert in the Basque Country despite coming from the Spanish region of Galicia. Traditional ingredients for this almond cake include ground almonds, eggs, sugar, and lemon zest. It has the recognizable Santiago Cross pattern and is frequently dusted with powdered sugar.

- **Txakoli**: While not a food item in and of itself, Txakoli is a typical white wine from the Basques that goes exceptionally well with the flavours of Basque cuisine. The Basque Country's coastline vineyards create this slightly effervescent, acidic wine, which is frequently paired with pintxos or shellfish dishes.

These regional specialties are just a sample of what the Basque Country has to offer in terms of culinary delights. The Basque cuisine offers a delectable tour through the region's history, culture, and culinary prowess with dishes ranging from substantial soups to grilled meats and decadent sweets.

Michelin-Starred Restaurants

The Basque Country is well known for its outstanding culinary scene and is home to several Michelin-starred eateries that have won praise from throughout the world. The following Basque Country restaurants have received Michelin stars, so you might want to check them out:

- **Arzak (San Sebastian):** San Sebastian is home to the illustrious three Michelin-star restaurant Arzak. The restaurant, run by Chef Juan Mari Arzak and his daughter Elena Arzak, is renowned for its avant-garde and inventive approach to Basque food. Arzak offers a distinctive dining experience that fuses conventional flavours with cutting-edge cooking methods.

- Azurmendi (Larrabetzu) is a three-Michelin-star restaurant run by Chef Eneko Atxa that is situated in a rural area close to Bilbao. It is recognized for its environmentally friendly and sustainable approach to gastronomy, using products that are sourced locally and boasting a gorgeous greenhouse where some of the produce is grown. The eatery provides a unique and engaging dining experience.

- In the municipality of Lasarte-Oria, which is close to San Sebastian, is the three-Michelin-star restaurant known as Martin Berasategui.

The restaurant, which is run by Chef Martin Berasategui, highlights his creative and exact cooking methods. International and Basque cuisines are combined on the menu to create a perfect fusion of culinary delights.

- Two Michelin stars are bestowed upon Mugaritz (Errenteria), which is close to San Sebastian. The culinary crew is led by Chef Andoni Luis Aduriz, who provides an exceptional dining experience.

Mugaritz specialises in experimental cuisine, pushing the limits of customary tastes and textures to produce dishes that surprise and astonish the senses.

- Getaria's coastal village of Elkano is home to the Michelin-starred Elkano restaurant. It specialises in seafood, especially grilled fish, and is renowned for its mastery of whole turbot preparation. Elkano makes a point of highlighting the freshness and quality of its ingredients, letting the tastes of the seafood stand out.

- **Etxebarri (Axpe):** Etxebarri, a restaurant in the Basque rural village of Axpe, has received one Michelin star. Victor Arguinzoniz, a chef famous for his proficiency in live-fire cooking methods, uses ingredients gathered locally to produce flavours that are firmly anchored in Basque culture.

  The restaurant's emphasis on grilled meats, fish, and veggies embodies simplicity and quality in its purest form.

These are only a few illustrations of the illustrious Basque Country Michelin-starred eateries. Each provides a distinctive dining experience that emphasises the area's extensive culinary history. These restaurants encourage you to experience a wonderful culinary trip in the Basque Country, featuring avant-garde concoctions and traditional flavours cooked with delicacy.

Local Markets and Food Festivals

Exploring the neighbourhood markets and food festivals is a great way to get a taste of the Basque Country's rich culinary heritage because of the region's well-known vibrant food culture. Here are a few famous Basque Country farmers' markets and culinary celebrations:

Regional Markets

- **San Sebastian's La Bretxa Market (in the city centre):** La Bretxa Market has a broad selection of fresh local produce, fish, meats, cheeses, and other foods. The best ingredients the Basque Country has to offer may be found in this crowded market, where you can browse and sample them.

- One of the biggest covered markets in Europe is located in Bilbao at Mercado de la Ribera. Fresh fruits, vegetables, meats, seafood, and authentic Basque items are all abundantly available. The market also has several bars and eateries where you can eat pintxos and regional cuisine.

- **Santo Tomás Market (San Sebastian):** The Old Town (Parte Vieja) of San Sebastian hosts the Santo Tomás Market on December 21st.

Local farmers and producers congregate at this traditional Christmas market to offer their wares, which include cheese, sausages, veggies, and cider. It's a wonderful chance to take in the festive mood and savour the seasonal delights.

Festivals of Food:

- **San Sebastian Gastronomika:**
  San Sebastian Gastronomika is a
  celebrated cuisine event that takes
  place there every year.
  Internationally renowned chefs,
  culinary experts, and food lovers
  congregate there.

  The festival offers lectures,
  workshops, and cooking
  demonstrations that highlight the
  most recent developments in the
  culinary industry.

- The Euskal Herriko Pintxo
  Txapelketa is an annual pintxos
  tournament that takes place in
  many places throughout the
  Basque Country and highlights the
  talent and originality of regional
  chefs. You may sample a variety of
  pintxos dishes and see the skill
  and passion that go into making

these tasty treats for little portions.

- Irun hosts the historical and cultural event known as Alarde de San Marcial every year. Despite not being a true culinary festival, it provides a rare chance to sample authentic Basque cuisine.

Large communal dinners made up of traditional Basque foods like marmitako, chorizo a la sidra, and cider are prepared during the festival by local groups.

- **Getaria Fishermen's Day (Getaria):** Getaria, a coastal community well-known for its seafood, honours its fishing heritage on this day. The celebration includes a variety of events, such as boat parades, fishing contests, and, naturally, the chance to sample freshly caught seafood served in traditional Basque fashions.

You may engage with the dynamic culinary culture of the Basque Country, speak with regional producers and chefs, and enjoy the flavours of this gastronomically diverse area by going to these local markets and food festivals.

For food enthusiasts and others interested in learning about the Basque Country's culinary gems, it is an unforgettable experience.

CULTURAL EXPERIENCES

The Basque Country is renowned for both its delectable gastronomy and its extensive cultural heritage. Following are some cultural activities you can take part in when visiting the Basque

Country:

- **Basque Pelota:** Basque Pelota is a long-standing sport that has a strong cultural foundation in the Basque nation. It can be thrilling and authentic to see a pelota match, in which participants strike a ball against a wall with a glove that resembles a handball. You can watch this thrilling sport on pelota courts in several locations throughout the Basque Country.

- **Basque Folklore & Music**: The Basque Country is home to a thriving folk music scene, and attending a traditional music or dance performance is a wonderful opportunity to get a sense of the local way of life. Look for festivals or gatherings that feature traditional Basque dances like the arrest and jota, as well as traditional music like the trinities (accordion) and txalaparta (percussion instrument).

- The Basque language, Euskara, is one of the oldest in Europe and has a rich cultural history. It is also known as the Euskal Herria.

Your ability to interact with the locals will improve if you learn a few simple phrases and get involved in the language. Search for language programs, workshops, or cultural establishments that provide information about the Basque language and its significance to the local identity.

- Rural Basque sports, sometimes referred to as Herri Kirolak, are a distinctive feature of Basque culture. These activities include rural weightlifting, wood chopping, and stone lifting.

It can be a wonderful cultural experience to witness these incredible feats of strength and ability, and some towns host traditional country sports championships.

- **Basque Museums:** The Basque Country is home to several museums that provide visitors with a look at the history, culture, and arts of the area. Explore the San Telmo Museum in San Sebastian, which focuses on Basque history and culture, or pay a visit to the Guggenheim Museum in Bilbao, which is renowned for its spectacular architecture and modern art shows. Famous Basque artists' works are displayed in other institutions including the Chillida-Leku Museum outside of San Sebastian and the Basque Museum in Bilbao.

- **Basque Festivals:** Basque celebrations, or "fiestas," play a significant role in the calendar of the area's cultural events. Parades, traditional dances, musical performances, and street parties are frequently part of these festivals.

The most well-known Basque festivals that provide a vibrant and comprehensive cultural experience include the Semana Grande in San Sebastian, the Aste Nagusia en Bilbao, and the San Fermin festival in Pamplona (famous for the running of the bulls).

- **Rural traditions in the Basque Country:** If you explore the countryside, you can see centuries-old customs, rural buildings, and traditional farming methods. Visit tiny towns and farms to experience Basque rural life, see how crafts are made, and sample regional foods like cheese, cider, and traditional bread.

You can have a greater understanding of the distinctive history and customs of the Basque Country by participating in these cultural events. You can get to know the people there, discover their history, and become engrossed in the region's fascinating cultural diversity.

Basques Culture and Traditions

The Basque people have a strong sense of identity and national pride, and their culture is vibrant and distinctive. The following are some significant facets of Basque customs and culture:

- **Language**: Euskara, the ancient and distinctive language of the Basques, predates the Indo-European languages. To maintain and advance the language, which is seen as an essential component of Basque identity, efforts have been made. Although Spanish is the primary language of the Basque Country, you might come across bilingual signs and overhear conversations in Euskara.

- **Basque Folklore and Music:** Basque folklore is an important component of the area's cultural heritage. Vibrant dances frequently accompany the traditional Basque music, which frequently includes instruments like the exist (flute) and alb oka (double-reed wind instrument). Traditional dances like the arrest and jota are performed by folklore groups called cantharis, exhibiting the vibrant and dynamic essence of Basque culture.

- Rural Basque sports, or Herri Kirolak, are a reflection of the area's long agricultural history. These activities include weightlifting in the countryside, woodchopping, tug-of-war, and stone lifting. They demonstrate the fortitude, tenacity, and ties to the soil of the Basque people.

- **Basque Festivals**: In cities and villages all around the Basque Country, basque festivals, or "fiestas," are observed year-round. These celebrations, which frequently centre around religious or historical occasions, are distinguished by colourful processions, live music, traditional dances, competitive sporting events, and delectable cuisine.

They provide a rare chance to experience the joy, friendliness, and cultural pride of the Basque people.

- **Basque food:** The quality and creativity of Basque food are well-known internationally. Fresh local foods, including seafood, meats, vegetables, and dairy products, are used in Basque cuisine.

The Basque equivalent of tapas, pintxos, is a gastronomic high point that emphasises the inventiveness and tastes of the area. Traditional Basque cuisine includes beloved favourites like txuletón (grilled beef), marmitako (fisherman's stew), and bacalao al pil-pil (salted cod).

- **Rural traditions in the Basque Country:** The Basque Country is deeply rooted in its rural past. Fishing, farming of sheep, and agriculture have all historically been significant economic activities. Many rural communities continue to celebrate and preserve old customs like sheepherding, manufacturing cheese, and making cider. You can tour rural farms, take part in customary pursuits, and eat real Basque fare.

- **Basque Identity and Autonomy:** The Basque Country possesses a strong feeling of regional identity and autonomy. There have been cries for Basque self-government and the preservation of Basque culture throughout history. Because the area has its administration, police force, and educational system, the Basque identity and language are preserved.

- The Basque people's daily lives are firmly rooted in Basque culture and traditions.

When you visit the Basque Country, learning more about these cultural features can help you gain a richer knowledge of the region's past, present, and national pride.

Festivals and Events

The Basque Country is renowned for its lively and varied celebrations of its cultural traditions and heritage. Here are a few important Basque Country celebrations and occasions:

- The Big Week, also known as Semana Grande (Aste Nagusia), is a significant festival that takes place in San Sebastian in August. In addition to live music performances, traditional Basque sports, fireworks displays, parades, and street performances are among the many events that are featured. Experience the vivid energy of the city at this fun-filled time.

- Bilbao's Aste Nagusia, or Great Week, is an annual celebration that takes place in August. The event lasts for a week and features street entertainment, musical performances, theatrical productions, bullfighting, and traditional Basque sports. The traditional txupinazo, in which a rocket is fired to signal the beginning of the festivities, is the festival's main attraction.

- **San Fermin - Pamplona:** The running of the bulls is a highlight of the San Fermin celebration in Pamplona. The festival, which takes place from July 6 to July 14, draws tens of thousands of tourists who come to see the adrenaline-fueled bull run through the streets of the city. The festival also features fireworks, processions, music, and dance.

- **Festival of Santo Tomas in San Sebastian:** On December 21st, San Sebastian hosts the Festival of Santo Tomas. Farmers and other producers congregate in the Old Town for this customary Christmas market to sell their wares. You can sample regional foods like cider, cheese, and sausages while taking in the festive ambiance.

- **Bilbao BBK Live - Bilbao:** In July, Bilbao hosts the well-known music festival known as Bilbao BBK Live. It includes well-known performers from several musical genres, both domestically and outside. Live music performances take place in a distinctive location at the festival, which is held on the mountainside of Mount Cobetas.

- San Sebastian's Jazzaldia is one of Europe's oldest jazz events and is also referred to as the San Sebastian Jazz Festival. It takes place in July and draws renowned jazz musicians and music fans from all around the world. A variety of concerts, jam sessions, and free outdoor performances are available during the festival.

- **Euskal Jaiak - Various Locations:** Throughout the Basque Country, cities and villages participate in Euskal Jaiak or Basque Festivals. These celebrations highlight the music, dance, athletics, and delectable cuisine of the Basques. Every town celebrates differently, giving visitors a chance to get a feel for the community.

These are only a handful of the numerous festivals and events that are held all year long in the Basque Country. By participating in these celebrations, you may experience the lively atmosphere, learn about customs from the past, take in live music performances, sample regional cuisine, and make long-lasting memories of the vibrant Basque culture.

Basque Pelota

Basque Pelota, often referred to as Euskal Pilota in Basque, is a long-standing activity with deep cultural roots in the Basque Country. It is a frantic, handball-like game played either indoors or outdoors on a fronton (pelota court) court against a wall. Following are some essential facts regarding Basque Pelota:

- **History**: Basque Pelota has a lengthy, several-century-old history. It is thought to have its roots in the Basque Country and has changed over time. The game was historically played in village squares as a form of entertainment and competition and has significant origins in Basque culture.

- Basque Pelota has several different game versions, each with its own set of rules and court configurations. Several well-liked versions include:

- **Handball (Remonte):** The most popular variation of Basque Pelota, played with a leather glove. Players use their gloved hands to strike the ball against the front wall.

- Played with a wooden paddle called a "pala," participants hit the ball against the front wall in this game. In rural places, this version is frequently played.

- **Cesta Punta**: A long, curved basket (cesta) that is fastened to the player's arm is used to play this game. The Cesta is used against the front wall to catch and throw the ball.

- **Xare**: In this classic version, players strike the ball against the front wall with a wooden racket called a "care." Although it is less popular, Xare is still played in some rural regions.

- **Fronton**: The specific court where Basque Pelota is played is called a fronton. Three walls are usually present, with one side exposed to spectators. In the Basque Country, frontons are common in towns and villages, and many of them regularly hold pelota contests and competitions.

- **Professional Players:** Basque Pelota has a system of professional leagues, and the sport's most accomplished players compete in these leagues. Professional pelotaris, as the players are known, put in a lot of practice to hone their abilities and compete in events throughout the Basque Country and beyond.

- Basque Pelota is strongly established in Basque cultural identity and has great cultural significance. It is more than just a sport.

  It is a symbol of Basque tradition and pride and stands for power, agility, and teamwork. The popularity of the sport has grown outside the Basque Country, as evidenced by the presence of contests and exhibits there.

Attending a Basque Pelota match is a thrilling event that gives you the chance to observe the players' agility, talent, and fervour. Whether you're a fan of sports or simply want to learn more about Basque culture, Basque Pelota provides a fascinating look into the region's customs and history.

Basque Language (Euskara)

The Basque Country, which includes sections of northern Spain and southwestern France, is home to the ancient and distinctive Euskara language, also known as the Basque language. What you need to know about the Basque language is as follows:

- **Unique Language:** Euskara is regarded as an isolated language, which means that it has no connections to any other languages that are currently known to exist. Since there are no recognized linguistic relations, it is one of the earliest languages in Europe.

- **Regional Language:** In the Basque Autonomous Community and several of the bordering territories, Basque is one of three co-official languages, along with Spanish (in Spain) and French (in

France). Basque is mostly spoken in the Basque Country, but there are also small populations of Basques all over the world.

- **Dialects:** The Basque Country is home to several dialects that fall under the umbrella term of "Euskara." The language is standardised in its most widely spoken dialect, Batua, which is derived from the core dialects. Gipuzkoan, Navarrese, and Bizkaian are a few other dialects.

- **Language Revitalization**: The Basque language has struggled throughout the years, including times when it was suppressed and ignored. However, initiatives to revive and promote the language have been successful, and interest in studying and using Euskara has increased. In addition to attempts to promote the use of the Basque language in daily life, schools offer instruction in the language.

- **Academies of the Basque Language:** The Euskaltzaindia (Royal Academy of the Basque Language) is the recognized body in charge of regulating and standardising the Basque language. It is essential for maintaining and growing the language, encouraging its usage, and building dictionaries and other language resources.

- **Daily Life in the Basque Country:** Even though Spanish is extensively used there, especially in metropolitan areas, the Basque language is still very present. Its usage and visibility are aided by bilingual signs, Basque-language media, and educational institutions.

- **Language and Culture of the Basques:** Euskara is essential for maintaining and expressing Basque cultural identity. Many cultural activities, works of literature, and artistic expressions are conducted in the Basque language, which is regarded as a sign of Basque heritage.

  The language is also embraced in traditional Basque music, dance, and folklore.

The chance to experience the Basque language directly is only available by travelling to the Basque Country. You can increase your awareness and appreciation of the area's rich linguistic and cultural legacy by conversing with people, picking up a few basic words, and going to cultural events in the Basque language.

Museums and Art Galleries

Numerous museums and galleries that highlight the rich cultural heritage, historical significance, and artistic expression of the Basque Country may be found there. Here are some noteworthy galleries and museums to visit:

- The Guggenheim Museum is an architectural wonder and a well-known art gallery that is situated in Bilbao. It has a sizable collection of modern and contemporary art, including pieces by notable creators including Andy Warhol, Jeff Koons, and Eduardo Chillida. The museum is a must-see sight because of its remarkable interior and exterior design.

- **San Telmo Museum:** The San Telmo Museum, located in the centre of San Sebastian's Old

Town, is devoted to Basque history and culture. With exhibitions on Basque art, archaeology, ethnography, and modern culture, it provides a fascinating tour through Basque heritage. The museum sheds light on the historical evolution, customs, and traditions of the area.

- **Bilbao Fine Arts Museum:** The Bilbao Fine Arts Museum is a prestigious gallery that has an exceptional collection of Basque, Spanish, and foreign artwork. Distinguished artists including El Greco, Goya, and Picasso have works on display for visitors to appreciate. The museum also puts on temporary exhibits and events, which enhance the visitor's exposure to art.

- **Chillida-Leku Museum:** The Chillida-Leku Museum honours renowned Basque sculptor Eduardo Chillida and is located in Hernani, close to San Sebastian. The museum is surrounded by a beautifully designed park and features some of Chillida's stunning sculptures. It provides a tranquil and compelling artistic experience.

- **Balenciaga Museum**: Located in Getaria, the Balenciaga Museum honours the town's native Cristóbal Balenciaga, an important fashion designer. The museum highlights Balenciaga's influence on the fashion industry and displays his inventive designs. It shows the development of Balenciaga's designs and gives a peek into the world of haute couture.
- Jorge Oteiza is the subject of the Oteiza Museum, which located in Alzuza, close to Pamplona. A

sizable collection of Oteiza's sculptures, paintings, and essays are on display at the museum, giving visitors a glimpse into his creative process and contributions to modern art.

- Basque Museum-Center of Contemporary Art, Artium, is a museum of modern and contemporary Basque art that is situated in Vitoria-Gasteiz. It includes exhibitions, installations, and multimedia displays that explore current artistic trends while showcasing the works of Basque artists.

These are only a few of the numerous museums and galleries in the Basque Country that provide a varied cultural experience. You can learn more about the art, history, and creative expression of the area by investigating these institutions, which will give you a better grasp of Basque culture and cultural legacy.

OUTDOOR
ADVENTURES

For nature lovers and thrill seekers, the Basque Country offers a choice of outdoor excursions and activities. Here are some outdoor activities you might want to take into account while you're there, from rocky coastlines to gorgeous mountains:

- **Hiking & Mountain Climbing**: The Basque Country is blessed with gorgeous scenery and a variety of topography, making these activities perfect there. You can stroll through verdant forests, visit the untamed shoreline, or scale the Pyrenean summits.

  The Gorbea Natural Park, the Urkiola Natural Park, and the Pyrenean trails close to the French border are also well-liked places to go hiking.

- **Surfing & water sports**: The Basque Country is a mecca for surfers thanks to its stunning beaches and top-notch waves. Zarautz, Mundaka, and Zurriola Beach in San Sebastian are well-known surfing locations.

  Along the seashore, you may also practise various water sports including windsurfing, kayaking, and paddleboarding.

- **Riding and Mountain Biking:** Both road cyclists and mountain bikers may find a network of riding routes in the Basque Country. You may bike along beautiful coastline routes, discover attractive country roads, or test your mettle on mountain riding paths. Old railroad tracks that have been transformed into bicycle routes are known as "Greenways" and offer a distinctive way to explore the area.

- **Rock Climbing:** There are many rock climbing locations in the Basque Country that are accessible to climbers of all skill levels. There are many alternatives for both conventional climbing and sport climbing, from coastal cliffs to inland crags. Atxarte, Baltzola, and Aralar Natural Park are popular locations.

- **Hang gliding and Paragliding**: Fly over the Basque landscapes while experiencing the exhilaration of flight and taking in the spectacular vistas. You can take lessons or fly in a tandem flight with a trained instructor at specified launch sites.
- **Sailing and boating**: Use a sailboat or a boat to explore the Basque coastline and its secret

bays. Rent a sailboat, catamaran, or motorboat to explore remote beaches, go fishing, or just take in the coastline's splendour from a new angle.

- **Animal Observation**: The Basque Country is home to a variety of flora and fauna, providing chances for animal lovers. Go to the Urdaibai Biosphere Reserve to see a variety of bird species, including migrating birds. Other great locations for birdwatching include the Txingudi Wetlands and the Aana Salt Flats.

Keep in mind to monitor the weather, abide by safety precautions, and, if required, hire knowledgeable guides or instructors for specific activities. The natural splendour of the Basque Country makes a beautiful setting for outdoor activities that enable you to connect with nature and develop lifelong memories.

Hiking And Nature Trails

The Basque Country has a stunning natural setting that is ideal for hiking and environmental exploration. Here are various hiking and nature trails to take into account, whether you prefer oceanfront strolls, mountain treks, or peaceful woodland paths:

- **Flysch Route (Zumaia):** This scenic coastline route leads you past the breathtaking cliffs of Zumaia, where you can see the rare flysch geological phenomenon. On the walk, you may discover gorgeous beaches and enjoy spectacular views of the rocky coastline.

- Gorbeia Natural Park is a hiking enthusiast's heaven and is situated between the provinces of Bizkaia and Araba. A number of paths are available in the park, including the well-liked climb up Mount

Gorbeia, the highest peak in the Basque Country. Beautiful vistas, highland meadows, and lush woods are all part of the varied terrain.

- **Oianleku Forest (Urkiola Natural Park):** The picturesque Urkiola Natural Park is home to a variety of plants and animals. The Oianleku Forest route offers a serene and all-encompassing nature experience as it leads you through historic beech and oak woodlands. The Oianleku viewpoint, which the walk takes you to, offers breathtaking panoramic views of the mountains in the area.

- The Bay of Biscay and the French shoreline are both visible from the Jaizkibel Coastal Path, which is close to Hondarribia. The route leads you along the Jaizkibel cliffs while passing through quaint fishing communities, monuments, and picturesque vistas. It's a wonderful way to take in the Basque Country's seaside splendour.

- Aizkorri-Aratz Natural Park is a paradise for nature enthusiasts and is situated in the provinces of Gipuzkoa and Alava. It has a system of hiking paths that take you through scenic valleys, rolling hills, and mountainous terrain. The park is well-known for its towering summits, such as Mount Aizkorri, which offers breathtaking 360-degree vistas.

- **Bizkaia's Anboto and Arrazola:** Climbing Mount Anboto is a strenuous but rewarding adventure. This trail winds through thick forests and steep terrain in the Urkiola

Mountain Range. The high point is climbing Anboto's summit, which gives breathtaking panoramas of the surroundings. You can stop by the lovely Arrazola beech forest on the route.

- Between Gipuzkoa and Navarre sits the calm and picturesque Aralar Natural Park, which offers a variety of hiking routes. The park's limestone mountains, extensive beech woods, and lovely meadows are its most notable features. There are many routes to discover, from simple strolls to strenuous hikes.

There are several hiking and wildlife routes in the Basque Country; here are just a few examples. Before starting any hiking expedition, make sure to always check the trail's condition, get maps or guides, and take the essential safety precautions. Experience the splendour of nature and the breathtaking scenery of the Basque Country.

Surfing and Water Sports

Due to its beautiful coastline and top-notch waves, the Basque Country is a well-known surfing and other water sport destination. Here are several locations and activities to enjoy, regardless of your level of surfing:

- One of the most well-known surfing spots in the Basque Country is Zarautz, which is in the Gipuzkoa province. For surfers at all skill levels, it provides reliable waves. There is plenty of room for everyone to enjoy the waves on the lengthy sandy beach. Along the promenade, you may locate surf schools and rental businesses.

- **Mundaka**: A renowned surfing location that draws surfers from all over the world to its world-class left-hand wave. An expert surfer's nirvana, the river mouth forms a sandbar that generates lengthy, hollow waves. It is significant to highlight that, in order to protect the ecosystem, access to the Mundaka wave is limited at specific periods of the year.

- San Sebastian's Zurriola Beach, which offers a thriving surf scene, is situated right in the middle of the city. All levels of surfers can use it because of its reliable beach break. Along the beach, there are surf schools and rental businesses, making it simple for newcomers to pick up the sport and enjoy it.

- **Sopelana**: This beach, which is close to Bilbao, is well known for its excellent waves and welcoming atmosphere for surfers. There are both left- and right-hand waves there, giving surfers with diverse tastes alternatives. Cliffs surround the shore, giving it a lovely backdrop.

- Stand-up paddleboarding (SUP) is becoming more and more popular in the Basque Country. You can practise this activity on the shore or in calmer bodies of water like rivers or estuaries. Paddleboarding is a fun and soothing water sport that lets you take in the splendour of the Basque coastline.

- Another great method to discover the Basque coast's secret coves and caves is via kayaking. Kayaks may be rented, and you can join guided trips to paddle around the coast, finding isolated beaches and admiring the beautiful scenery from the water.

- **Windsurfing:** The Basque Country provides excellent prospects for windsurfing due to its ideal wind conditions. Popular windsurfing locations include

Zarautz, Hondarribia, and Lekeitio. Both novice and expert windsurfers can use the rental facilities and schools there.

Be sure to verify the local tides, weather, and surf reports before venturing out, and make sure you have the skills and gear required for the sport you select.

The Basque Country offers a great backdrop for surfing and a variety of thrilling water sports experiences, whether you're learning to surf or hone your talents.

Scenic Driving and Coastal Exploration

The Basque Country is a fantastic location for scenic drives and coastal exploration because it is endowed with beautiful scenery and a magnificent coastline. Here are some picturesque seaside roads and locations to explore:

- **Basque Coast Geopark**: From Mutriku to Zumaia, the coastline is covered by the Basque Coast Geopark. Incredibly beautiful cliffs, untamed rock formations, and amazing coastline views may be found at this UNESCO-designated geopark. Explore the quaint coastal towns and villages as you travel down the meandering coastal route, making viewpoint stops along the way.

- San Juan de Gaztelugatxe is a lovely islet with a mediaeval hermitage situated on top that can be found close to Bermeo. The islet is connected to the mainland by a little stone bridge, which provides a singular experience. Drive along the coast to San Juan de Gaztelugatxe, where you may trek up to the hermitage for sweeping views of the sea.

- **Getaria**: This quaint seaside community is well known for its scenic harbour, its winding alleyways, and its stunning beaches. Drive along the coast to Getaria, where you may stroll through the old part of the city and take in the breathtaking sea views. Don't pass up the opportunity to sample the regional delicacy, grilled fish, at one of the seaside eateries.

- **Orio**: Located near the Oria River's mouth, Orio is a picturesque fishing community renowned for its lovely beach and quaint old town. To experience Orio, take the coastal route there, wander along the promenade, and take in the seaside ambiance. At the town's renowned eateries, you may also eat fresh fish.

- **Flysch Route (Zumaia to Deba):** The Flysch Route is a spectacular seaside trail that connects Zumaia and Deba and provides breathtaking views of the flysch rock formations along the way. The distinctive geological formations that have been carved by the water over millions of years can be seen as you travel along the coastal route and halt at designated viewpoints.

- Hondarribia is a lovely coastal town with a well-preserved mediaeval section that is close to the French border. Explore

Hondarribia's winding alleys, old structures, and scenic harbour by driving along the coast. The town is a joy to visit because of its vibrant houses and coastline views.

- **Lekeitio**: This seaside community is well-known for its lovely beach, quaint old town, and bustling fishing port. Visit Lekeitio by taking the coastal route, exploring its winding lanes, and stopping at the Basilica of Santa Maria, which looks out over the town and provides sweeping ocean views.

These are just a few of the beautiful coastline areas and winding roads in the Basque Country. As you explore the area's hidden gems and little seaside communities, take your time, relish the coastline splendour, and immerse yourself in its breathtaking vistas.

Parks and Gardens

There are several parks and gardens in the Basque Country where you may unwind, take in the scenery, and enjoy nature. Here are several well-known green spaces to visit:

- **Cristina Enea Park (San Sebastian):** Cristina Enea Park is a serene oasis offering a peaceful getaway from the busy city. It is situated in the centre of San Sebastian. The park has rich vegetation, winding walks, a tiny lake, and lovely gardens. It's the ideal location for a tranquil stroll or a picnic in the great outdoors.

- Alderdi Eder Park in San Sebastian is a well-liked gathering place for locals and tourists. It is located close to La Concha Beach. Beautiful views of the harbour and the city's famous monuments may be found at the park. It's the perfect area to relax and take in the coastal atmosphere with well-kept lawns, vibrant flower beds, and comfortable benches.

- The Bilbao park known as Parque de Dona Casilda is a sizable urban park that features lovely gardens, a lake, sculptures, and walking trails. A wide variety of plant species, including uncommon and exotic plants, can be found in the park. It's a tranquil and lovely location to take a leisurely stroll or unwind in nature.

- Arriaga Park in Bilbao is a green area that provides a tranquil retreat in the middle of the city and is located close to the Guggenheim Museum Bilbao. The park has a centre pond, flowerbeds, and walks bordered with trees. It's the perfect place to unwind, read a book, or just take in the scenery.

- **Parque Natural de Urkiola:** The Urkiola Natural Park is a sizable protected area that includes mountains, forests, and meadows and is situated between the provinces of Bizkaia and Araba. The park has a ton of vistas, picnic spots, and hiking routes. It offers opportunities for birdwatching, wildlife viewing, and total immersion in the pristine natural surroundings, making it a haven for nature lovers.

- **Santa Catalina Park (Irun):** Santa Catalina Park is a charming green area with lovely gardens, fountains, and play areas. It is located in the town of Irun. The park has a calm environment and is ideal for family outings or leisurely strolls.

- **Parque Europa (Vitoria-Gasteiz):** In this unusual park in Vitoria-Gasteiz, visitors can see scaled-down versions of well-known European landmarks. It provides strolling trails, ponds, and gardens that are kept up properly. Visitors can explore the little reproductions while taking in the beauty of the gardens, making for an entertaining and instructive experience.

These gardens and parks offer peaceful settings for unwinding, getting in touch with nature, and taking in the splendour of the Basque Country. These green areas provide a pleasant getaway from the urban bustle, whether you're looking for peace & quiet, a place to decompress, or a scenic setting for a leisurely walk.

DAY TRIPS AND EXCURSIONS

Due to its convenient location, the Basque Country makes several exciting day trips and excursions easily accessible. Some ideas for day trips from San Sebastian and other significant regional cities are provided below:

- Discover the dynamic city of Bilbao, home of the renowned Guggenheim Museum Bilbao, which features cutting-edge artwork and eye-catching architecture. Visit the famed pintxo bars and eateries in the city, stroll along the Nervion River, and see the historic Casco Viejo (Old Town).

- Visit the upscale beach town of Biarritz in France by crossing the border. Biarritz provides a distinctive fusion of French and

Basque elements and is well known for its stunning beaches, surf culture, and opulent resorts. Take it easy by the water, see the town's exquisite architecture, and indulge in some delectable French fare.

- **Pamplona**: Attend the renowned Running of the Bulls festival (San Fermin), which takes place there every July. Explore the city's historic core, which has spectacular mediaeval walls, charming streets, and lively squares, or go to the heart-pounding event.

- Explore the Rioja Wine Region, which is renowned for producing some of Spain's best wines, on a wine-tasting excursion. Learn about the winemaking process while touring vineyards and wineries and tasting a selection of reds and whites. The cities of Haro and Laguardia are excellent places to start your exploration of the area.

- Discover the French side of the Basque Country by travelling to quaint cities like Saint-Jean-de-Luz and Bayonne. Discover their charming alleyways, sample French Basque specialties, and take in the distinctive fusion of Basque and French culture.

- **Gaztelugatxe**: Visit the charming islet of Gaztelugatxe by travelling along the rocky shoreline close to Bermeo. Reach the hermitage located atop the island by ascending the twisting stone steps, and you'll be rewarded with breathtaking views of the surrounding sea and countryside.

- Hondarribia is a charming village with a well-preserved mediaeval district that isn't too far from San Sebastian. Discover its quaint fishing port, meander through its winding alleyways, and dine at nearby establishments to sample authentic Basque cuisine.

- Travel to the magnificent hermitage of San Juan de Gaztelugatxe, which is close to Bakio. This islet offers amazing views of the coastline and a distinctive spiritual environment and is reached by a stone bridge.

These are only a few of the numerous day-trip possibilities offered in the Basque Country. The area provides a wide variety of attractions that are convenient for enjoyable day outings, whether your interests are cultural exploration, outdoor adventures, or gastronomic experiences.

Bilbao: Guggenheim Museum and More

The largest city in the Basque Country, Bilbao, is a pulsating centre of culture with a fascinating past and a thriving art scene. Even while the renowned Guggenheim Museum is a must-see site, there is a lot more to see in this vibrant city. The following highlights:

- Starting your day in Bilbao with a visit to the famed Guggenheim Museum is a great way to start the city. The museum, a Frank Gehry architectural marvel, displays a sizable collection of modern and contemporary art. Discover the eye-catching exhibits, adore the titanium-clad curves of the exterior, and savour the breathtaking Nervion River views.

- **Casco Viejo (Old Town):** After immersing yourself in modern art, visit Bilbao's quaint Old Town at

Casco Viejo. Explore the neighbourhood's small, traditional-building-lined streets while strolling, and stop at the Plaza Nueva, which is historically significant. Try pintxos, the Basque equivalent of tapas, at one of the many bars in the area.

- The Bilbao Fine Arts Museum should be visited if you have a penchant for classical art. The museum is home to a sizable collection of European and Spanish artwork from the Middle Ages to the present. Admire the creations of famous artists like El Greco, Goya, and Picasso.

- **Euskalduna Palace:** Take a tour of this modern conference and performing arts venue that's close to the Guggenheim Museum. Concerts, plays, and exhibitions are just a few of the cultural events held at this architectural marvel.

- **Ribera Market:** Enjoy the lively ambiance of one of Europe's largest covered markets, the Mercado de la Ribera. Explore the vendors selling local specialties, fresh produce, and Basque fare. It's a terrific spot to get a taste of the local cuisine and some mouth watering sweets.

- Take a ride on the Artxanda Funicular for breathtaking panoramic views of Bilbao. You may ascend Mount Artxanda via a funicular railway and take in breathtaking views of the surrounding mountains, river, and city below. At the summit, there are cafes and restaurants where you may unwind and enjoy the view.

- **Maritime Museum:** The Maritime Museum, housed in the former Euskalduna shipyard, provides information about Bilbao's maritime history. Through interactive exhibits and displays, the museum highlights the history of sailing and shipbuilding in the city.

These are only a few of the highlights of Bilbao. The city is a mesmerising destination for art fans, history buffs, and food lovers equally thanks to its blend of modern architecture, cultural attractions, and culinary pleasures.

Biarritz: French Charm on the Coast

On the French side of the Basque Country, the lovely coastal town of Biarritz offers a delightful fusion of unspoiled landscapes, tasteful architecture, and a relaxed atmosphere. The following are some sights to see in Biarritz:

- Biarritz is renowned for its beautiful beaches, which draw surfers and sun worshippers from all over the world. Golden beaches and magnificent views of the Hôtel du Palais may be seen at the town's primary beach, Grande Plage. Visit Plage de la Côte des Basques, a stunning section of the coastline renowned for its exceptional surf conditions, for a more laid-back vibe.

- The majestic palace-turned-hotel known as the Hôtel du Palais is a reminder of Biarritz's opulent past. The Hôtel du Palais, which Napoleon III built for his wife, Empress Eugénie, exudes luxury and provides stunning views of the Atlantic Ocean. You can still appreciate the hotel's facade and wander along the neighbouring promenade even if you aren't staying there.

- Immerse yourself in the oceanic environment at the Biarritz Aquarium. This fun family destination features a wide variety of aquatic life, including sharks, rays, and vibrant fish. Through engaging exhibitions and instructive displays, discover the significance of ocean conservation as well as the local marine ecosystem.

- **Les Halles Market**: Enjoy the lively ambiance of this covered market in Biarritz. A wide variety of local fresh products, regional delicacies, and gourmet foods are available here. Browse the vendors, eat the delectable cheeses and pastries, and purchase some trinkets to preserve the local flavours.

- **Rocher de la Vierge:** Reach Rocher de la Vierge, a rock formation featuring a statue of the Virgin Mary at its summit, by taking a stroll down the seashore. Take the walkway up to the rock, where you may marvel at the thundering waves against the cliffs and take in expansive views of the Bay of Biscay.

- **Biarritz Lighthouse**: Climb the lighthouse's steps to get sweeping views of the town, its beaches, and the nearby coastline. The lighthouse in Biarritz is still in use and acts as a significant landmark.

- **Rue du Port Vieux:** Stroll through the quaint, pedestrian-only streets of Rue du Port Vieux, which are dotted with eateries, cafes, and stores. Enjoy the laid-back vibe of this lovely promenade while perusing the boutiques and dining on delectable seafood.

With its lovely beaches, opulent buildings, and friendly environment, Biarritz perfectly encapsulates the essence of French charm on the coast. Biarritz offers a lovely getaway and a taste of the carefree coastal lifestyle, regardless of whether you love the beach, are interested in history, or are a foodie.

Hondarribia: A Mediaeval Gem

Hondarribia, often referred to as Fuenterrabia, is a charming village situated close to the French border on the Basque Country's eastern coast.

Hondarribia provides a riveting look into the history and beauty of the area with its well-preserved mediaeval quarter, attractive streets, and breathtaking sea vistas. The following are some attractions to check out in Hondarribia:

- Walk through the winding streets of Hondarribia's historic district, known as La Marina, to experience a step back in time. The neighbourhood is distinguished by its bright Basque and Gothic-style homes with wooden balconies, cobblestone lanes, and quaint squares. Explore the town's central

Plaza de Armas and take in the 15th-century Santa Maria Church.

- Visit the impressive Castle of Charles V, a stronghold constructed in the tenth century to protect the town from attacks. Discover the history of the area by climbing the towers for sweeping views, exploring the ramparts, and seeing the castle's exhibitions and displays.

- The Paseo Butrón is a promenade that provides stunning views of the Bay of Biscay and the town's shoreline. Enjoy a stroll along it. Admire the yachts at the marina, take in the picturesque surroundings, and take in the cool sea breeze.

- Explore Calle Mayor, the town's main thoroughfare, which is dotted with quaint Basque homes, businesses, and eateries. Take a look around the neighbourhood shops, try some Basque food, and take in the colourful atmosphere of this lively street.

- Visit Plaza de Guipúzcoa, a lovely square located in the centre of Hondarribia. This bustling area is a favourite gathering spot for both locals and tourists and is bordered by historical structures. Sit back and unwind at one of the outdoor cafes as you take in the scenery and people-watch.

- **Beaches**: Hondarribia has lovely sandy beaches where you can unwind and take in the coastline. The lovely Playa de Hondarribia offers a setting with views of the castle and is close to the ancient town. Across the border in France, Playa de Hendaya is conveniently located and boasts a lengthy expanse of golden sand.

- Visit the Maritime Museum to learn more about Hondarribia's maritime past. The museum is housed in a former home of a fisherman and features displays on fishing methods, nautical customs, and the significance of the sea to the community.

- The mediaeval allure, magnificent architecture, and coastline allure of Hondarribia make it a hidden gem well worth discovering. Hondarribia offers a pleasant getaway to a bygone age, whether you're meandering through its old streets, indulging in regional food, or just taking in the laid-back environment.

Getaria: Birthplace of Juan Sebastian Elcano

Juan Sebastián Elcano was born in Getaria, a picturesque seaside town in the Basque Country, and it is significant historically because he was the first person to circumnavigate the globe.

Getaria, which is situated on the Bay of Biscay, offers a scenic environment, an extensive maritime history, and delicious gastronomic delights. The following are some sights to see in Getaria:

- Visit the Juan Sebastián Elcano Museum, which is devoted to the life and explorations of the legendary explorer. Find more about Elcano's participation in Ferdinand Magellan's expedition and his amazing accomplishment of completing the first circumnavigation of the globe.

Elcano and his voyages are chronicled in the museum's relics, interactive exhibits, and historical information.

- **Old Town:** Take a stroll around Getaria's Old Town, which is distinguished by its mediaeval architecture and winding lanes. Explore the historic district, take in the charming Basque architecture, and take in the ambiance of this small fishing town.

- **Church of San Salvador**: In the centre of Getaria, this stunning Gothic-style church is worth a visit. Admire its exquisite architecture before entering to see the peaceful interior and holy artwork.

- **Getaria Port:** Wander along the Getaria Port and take in the vibrant fishing boats that are constantly bobbing in the water. Take in the picturesque views of the bay while taking in the marine ambiance and watching the fisherman unload their catch.

- Getaria is well known for being the birthplace of renowned fashion designer Cristóbal Balenciaga. Balenciaga Museum. Visit the Balenciaga Museum to learn more about his life and legacy. The museum showcases a variety of Balenciaga's notable creations, showing his ground-breaking contributions to the fashion industry.

- Getaria is well-known for producing Txakoli, a crisp white wine that is exclusive to the Basque Country. Visit some of the nearby wineries and vineyards to sample several Txakoli kinds, learn about the winemaking process, and take in the breathtaking views of the hills covered in vines.

- **Playa de Getaria:** Playa de Getaria is a lovely sandy beach close to the town centre, where you may unwind. Enjoy a stroll along the shoreline, a plunge in the cool waves, or some sun.

Getaria is an intriguing place to explore because of its historical significance, natural beauty, and culinary delights. Getaria offers a distinctive and unforgettable experience, regardless of your interests in fashion, wine tasting, maritime history, or simply taking in the seaside environment.

Pamplona: The Running of the Bulls

In the Spanish province of Navarre, Pamplona is best known for its annual San Fermin celebration, which includes the exhilarating Running of the Bulls (encierro).

Numerous tourists from all over the world flock to this age-old custom. Pamplona, though, has a lot more to offer than just the heart-pounding spectacle. Here are some of Pamplona's highlights to check out:

- Experience the thrill of the San Fermin Festival, which is held annually from July 6 to July 14. Watch as participants in the Running of the Bulls sprint with the animals through the Pamplona streets. Wear traditional white apparel and a red scarf to the celebrations and take part in the lively environment of music, dancing, and cultural events.

- Visit Plaza del Castillo, Pamplona's central square, and a popular gathering spot for both locals and tourists. Take a stroll, unwind at a café outside, and take in the bustling scene. The area is a great place to start exploring the city because it is surrounded by old buildings, shops, and eateries.

- **Pamplona Cathedral:** Take a tour of the majestic Pamplona Cathedral, a masterpiece of Gothic and Baroque architecture. Admire the finely crafted exterior before entering to take in the breathtaking interior, which includes the crypt and superb choir stalls. Don't pass up the chance to ascend the cathedral's tower for sweeping views of the area.

- Ciudadela Park is a green haven in the middle of Pamplona, where you can escape the bustle of the city. This vast park offers tranquil surroundings, lovely plants, and walking routes. It's the perfect location for outdoor recreation, a picnic, and relaxation.

- Visit the Museum of Navarra to learn more about the history and culture of the area. The museum is housed in a former hospital and features an extensive collection of ethnographic, fine art, and archaeological objects. Learn about the history of Navarre, from the beginning to the present.

- **Bullring Museum:** The Bullring Museum, situated in the Plaza de Toros de Pamplona, offers information on the history of bullfighting. Discover the historical and artistic bullfighting exhibitions at the museum, which feature costumes, images, and artefacts. For an inside look at this contentious activity, you may also go on a guided tour of the bullring.

- Discover the spectacular Citadel of Pamplona, a fortification from the 16th century that has been wonderfully conserved. Explore the citadel's underground tunnels, stroll along its ramparts, and discover its military past.

  Green spaces and lovely walking trails can be found in the neighbourhood park.

The San Fermin Festival and the Running of the Bulls may be Pamplona's most well-known attractions, but the city is a fascinating place to visit all year round because of its fascinating history, gorgeous architecture, and cultural activities. Pamplona has a lot to offer, whether you're looking for adventure, cultural encounters, or just a taste of Spanish charm.

SHOPPING AND ENTERTAINMENT

San Sebastian provides a wide variety of possibilities for shopping and entertainment to accommodate all interests and preferences. Here are some noteworthy points to consider:

- **Retail Districts:** Explore the city's retail areas to find a range of regional boutiques, upscale clothing stores, and global brands. Avenida de la Libertad, Calle San Marcial, and Calle Urbieta are some of the prominent shopping avenues. Explore these regions to find anything from specialty shops selling regional goods and souvenirs to fashion and accessory stores.

- **La Bretxa Market:** Visit this bustling indoor market in the heart of the city to take in its energetic atmosphere. You can browse a variety of fresh fruit, regional cheeses, meats, seafood, and other delectable foods here. Take advantage of the chance to talk to local merchants and sample Basque Country cuisine.

- **Retail Centers:** San Sebastian is home to several retail centres, including Centro Comercial Garbera and Centro Comercial Urbil, if you prefer a more contemporary shopping experience. Under one roof, these centres offer a range of shops, eateries, and entertainment venues.

- Take a stroll along the well-known La Concha Promenade, which runs alongside the stunning La Concha Bay. Enjoy the beautiful scenery, take in the ambiance, and perhaps pay a visit to the street stalls selling homemade goods and mementos.

- **Cinemas and theatres:** San Sebastian has a thriving cultural scene, and the city is home to several cinemas and theatres that provide a variety of entertainment alternatives. For plays, concerts, and other live entertainment, check out the schedule at Teatro Principal or Teatro Victoria Eugenia.

The city is home to the famed San Sebastian International Film Festival, which draws famous actors and directors from all over the world.

- San Sebastian is renowned for having a vibrant nightlife. There are several restaurants, taverns, and clubs in the Parte Vieja (Old Town) and neighbouring regions where you can go out with friends. As you take in the vibrant ambiance, try pintxos, the well-known Basque tapas, and drink regional wines and creative cocktails.

- Visit Casino Kursaal, which is close to Zurriola Beach, if you're feeling lucky. Slot machines, roulette, and poker tables are just a few of the games available in this contemporary casino. You may still enjoy the casino's entertainment and dining options even if you're not a gambler.

San Sebastian offers a variety of modern and traditional shopping options as well as a thriving entertainment scene. The city has something to offer for everyone, whether you're looking for one-of-a-kind mementos, cultural events, or a night of fun and excitement.

Shopping Streets and Districts

There are various shopping avenues and areas in San Sebastian where you may discover a wide variety of stores, boutiques, and shops. Here are a few of the city's well-known shopping districts:

- One of San Sebastian's main thoroughfares for shopping is the Avenida de la Libertad. There are a variety of high-end fashion boutiques, global brands, and regional specialty shops there. Along this lively avenue, there are numerous alternatives for footwear, apparel, and accessories.

- Calle San Marcial is a well-liked retail strip with a wide selection of stores that are situated in the heart of the city. You can find a variety of alternatives to fit all interests and price ranges, from apparel and shoes to jewellery and home décor. For even more retail options, explore the side streets that are connected to Calle San Marcial.

- **Calle Urbieta:** Calle Urbieta is a popular shopping avenue in San Sebastian that attracts both national and international retailers. There are a range of specialty businesses, shoe stores, and fashion boutiques to choose from. Explore the stores that catch your eye as you wander gently down Calle Urbieta.

- **Centro Comercial Garbera**: Centro Comercial Garbera is the place to go if you enjoy shopping malls. This contemporary mall, which is close to the city's core, has a variety of stores, including clothing stores, electronics stores, and salons and spas. Additionally, it has a movie theatre and many food alternatives.

- Another well-known shopping mall worth seeing is Centro Comercial Urbil, which is located in the nearby town of Usurbil. It has a wide variety of shops, including those for clothing, accessories, household items, and technology.

  The mall also has a variety of culinary establishments and entertainment alternatives.

- **Parte Vieja (Old Town):** The Old Town offers distinctive shopping opportunities in addition to its historic appeal and culinary treats. Explore the boutique stores selling regional handicrafts, handmade goods, gourmet foods, and Basque mementos throughout the Parte Vieja's winding streets. This neighbourhood is wonderful for browsing and shopping because it is very busy during the day.

There is something for every consumer in San Sebastian's shopping streets and neighbourhoods, which provide a mix of national and international brands. These locations offer a wide variety of possibilities to explore and delight in, whether you're seeking stylish clothing, handcrafted goods, or distinctive gifts.

Local Markets and Souvenirs

San Sebastian is renowned for its thriving local markets, where you can purchase seasonal vegetables, tasty treats from the region, and one-of-a-kind trinkets. Here are a few of the city's best markets:

- La Bretxa Market is a bustling indoor market that sells a wide range of goods and is situated in the centre of San Sebastian. Explore the booths selling native Basque specialties including fresh fruits, vegetables, seafood, meats, and cheeses.

  Additionally, specialty stores that sell gourmet products including wine, spices, chocolates, and olive oil can be found. Don't pass up the chance to sample some of the local cuisine.

- Mercado San Martin is a well-known market with a buzzing ambiance and high-quality goods that are located in the Parte Vieja (Old Town).

  Explore the booths selling local cheeses, fresh produce, artisanal goods, and traditional Basque delicacies. Enjoy the lively atmosphere and talk to the welcoming sellers to find out more about the regional culinary tradition.

- Gros Market is a bustling market that highlights the variety of regional goods and produce. It is situated in the Gros district. Explore the vendors selling local delicacies, baked products, fresh produce, and fruits. Visitors can enjoy the market's periodic activities, which include food fairs and cookery demonstrations, which are held there.

- **Alameda del Boulevard Market:** This market is held every Thursday along San Sebastian's lovely Alameda del Boulevard. Explore a variety of stalls selling clothing, accessories, crafts, artwork, and other items. It's a terrific location to find handmade goods, original souvenirs, and regional artisan crafts.

San Sebastian provides a variety of souvenir choices that showcase the history and culture of the city. Here are some well-liked mementos to think about:

- **Basque Txapela:** The "txapela," or traditional Basque beret, is a well-known emblem of the Basque Country. It makes for a distinctive and fashionable memento that you may wear or show off.

- **Basque Handicrafts**: Look for regional handicrafts such as textiles, woodwork, ceramics, and pottery. These products exhibit the region's aesthetic and craftsmanship traditions.

- Local foods like artisanal chocolates, olive oil, classic Basque sauces (like piquillo pepper sauce), and gourmet preserves are great ways to bring a taste of San Sebastian back home.

- San Sebastian is well-known for its manufacturing of Basque cider. Think about bringing some Basque cider home as a memento or a present for cider lovers.

- San Sebastian is home to a strong art scene. Find one-of-a-kind artwork, including paintings, sculptures, and prints from regional artists, by browsing art galleries and boutiques.

Don't forget to browse the neighbourhood markets, specialty stores, and boutiques to find more keepsakes that encapsulate San Sebastian and the Basque Country.

Nightlife San Sebastian

San Sebastian offers a thriving nightlife scene with a variety of options to accommodate all tastes. The city provides something for everyone, whether you're searching for a relaxing evening with friends, live music, or dancing till the early hours. Here are some of San Sebastian's nightlife highlights:

- **Parte Vieja (Old Town):** San Sebastian's vibrant nightlife is centred in the historic Parte Vieja. Numerous bars, taverns, and pintxos (Basque tapas) eateries may be found here.

  Explore the small alleyways and visit several bars while sampling mouthwatering pintxos and sipping regional beverages like txakoli (Basque white wine) or a cool gin & tonic.

- Another popular area for nightlife in San Sebastian is the Gros neighbourhood. It is renowned for having a lively environment and offering a variety of bars and clubs. You may discover hip bars and music establishments with live music acts, DJ sets, and a bustling atmosphere in Plaza Catalunya and the streets nearby.

- **Paseo de la Concha:** At night, bars and restaurants along La Concha Beach come alive, providing breathtaking views of the bay. Take a stroll down the waterfront, indulge in a drink at one of the seaside bars or restaurants, and take in the stunning scenery.

- Surfers frequent the beautiful beach of Zurriola, which also boasts a thriving nightlife. You may discover bars and clubs along the seashore where there is live music, DJ sessions, and a younger crowd. It's a terrific place to unwind, mingle, and enjoy the beachy atmosphere.

- **Jazz and music venues**: The jazz scene in San Sebastian is well-known. To see live jazz performances by regional and international musicians, go to jazz venues like Jazzaldia or La Casa de la Musica. Throughout the year, the city also holds some music festivals with a wide variety of musical styles, including rock, electronic music, jazz, and blues.

- If you're feeling lucky, stop by Casino Kursaal, which is close to Zurriola Beach. Slot machines, roulette, and poker tables are just a few of the games available in this contemporary casino. It also has a bar and restaurant on the premises and occasionally organises live entertainment events.

- Numerous cultural events and festivals are held in San Sebastian, many of which last well into the evening. There is always something going on in the city, from film festivals to music events to customary holidays. If there are any special events, such as performances or parties, scheduled during your visit, check the event calendar.

Every taste is catered for by the variety of classic and contemporary venues available in San Sebastian's nightlife. There are many ways to enjoy the city's bustling and exciting nightlife, whether you like a leisurely evening with friends, live music performances, or dancing the night away.

Theatres and Concert Hall

Numerous theatres and concert venues can be found in San Sebastian, where a range of events are presented, including plays, musicals, concerts of classical music, and modern performances. Here are some of the city's notable locations:

- One of San Sebastian's most prominent theatres is Teatro Victoria Eugenia, which is situated in the city's centre. Numerous performances are held in this historic location, including operas, concerts, dance performances, plays, musicals, and musicals. Cultural events can be held there in a compelling environment because of its stunning design and acoustics.

- **Teatro Principal**: Another notable theatre in San Sebastian is located close to the Old Town. It offers a varied schedule of theatrical works, including dramas, comedies, and appearances by both domestic and foreign theatre companies. The theatre also occasionally holds musical performances and film screenings.

- The Kursaal Congress Center and Auditorium is a strikingly modern structure that overlooks La Zurriola Beach. The Auditorium and the Chamber Hall, two concert halls with outstanding acoustics, are included. Numerous performances are held in Kursaal, including classical music concerts, presentations featuring modern music, dance performances, and theatrical productions.

- Tabakalera is a cultural hub that features a variety of artistic mediums, such as theatre, film, modern art, and multimedia installations. It is located in a former tobacco factory. Theatre productions, movie screenings, workshops, and other artistic events are frequently held there. The unique and experimental approach to the arts that Tabakalera employs is well known.

- Gaztetxea is a musical venue in the Egia area that specialises in modern music, especially rock, pop, and alternative genres. It provides a stage for up-and-coming artists and hosts performances by regional and international musicians. The lively ambiance of Gaztes Zena makes it a favourite hangout for music fans.

- **San Telmo Museoa:** Despite being primarily a museum, San Telmo Museoa also hosts concerts, plays, and lectures on occasion. With its blend of old and new, it offers a distinctive backdrop for artistic and intellectual events.

- **Festival locations**: San Sebastian is well-known for its festivals, which include the Jazzaldia Jazz Festival and the San Sebastian International Film Festival. Numerous locations throughout the city, including the Kursaal, Teatro Victoria Eugenia, and outdoor stages, are turned into vibrant settings for performances, films, and concerts during these festivities.

These theatres and concert venues add to San Sebastian's vibrant cultural landscape by providing chances to see a variety of artistic productions. To learn about forthcoming performances at these locations during your visit, check their event calendars and program listings.

Casino Kursaal

In San Sebastian, Spain, there is a well-known entertainment complex called Casino Kursaal. The following details pertain to Casino Kursaal:

- **Overview**: Casino Kursaal is a cutting-edge, fashionable casino that provides a wide range of gaming, entertainment, and eating opportunities. It is located close to Zurriola Beach and has grown to be recognized as a landmark.

- **Gaming:** The casino offers a variety of games for patrons to enjoy. A variety of slot machines with different themes and denominations are available. Additionally, there are tables for traditional casino games including baccarat, blackjack, poker, and roulette. The casino offers both seasoned gamblers and those eager to try their luck for the first time a dynamic and energetic atmosphere.

- Events and entertainment: Throughout the year, Casino Kursaal also hosts several events and entertainment programs. This includes themed events, live comedy shows, live music acts, and special promos. To find out what's going on when you're there, check the casino's events schedule.

- **Restaurant and Bar:** The casino has a bar and a restaurant where you can unwind and eat or drink. The bar serves a variety of beverages, such as cocktails, wines, and spirits. The restaurant offers a wide selection of food, from regional specialties to international fare. It's a wonderful location to unwind and eat before or after a gaming session.

- The dress code at Casino Kursaal is sophisticated and casual. Although wearing a suit or tie is not required, it is advised to look presentable and refrain from donning athletic or beachwear.

- **Gaming responsibly:** The casino encourages responsible gambling and offers support to individuals who might require it. They provide guidelines for responsible gaming and have safeguards in place to provide a secure and enjoyable gambling experience.

- You should check the casino's official website or get in touch with them directly for the most recent information because the availability of particular games, events, and food options can change.

Visitors visiting San Sebastian have an interesting entertainment option at Casino Kursaal, which combines gambling, dining, and live entertainment in a chic and contemporary setting. The casino offers a vibrant atmosphere for a great experience, whether you're an experienced gambler or just seeking a fun night out.

PRACTICAL INFORMATION

Certainly! Here are some useful tips to make the most of your trip to San Sebastian:

- **Currency**: The Euro (€) is the country's legal tender across Spain, including San Sebastian. For modest purchases, it's a good idea to have some cash on hand, but most businesses take credit and debit cards.

- Spanish is the city of San Sebastian's official language. However, the region also has speakers of Euskara, a Basque language. In tourist areas, hotels, restaurants, and stores, English is frequently understood and spoken.

- Central European Time (CET), which is UTC+1 in standard time, is observed in San Sebastian. The city observes Central European Summer Time (CEST), which is UTC+2, during daylight saving time.

- San Sebastian has an electrical voltage of 220-240 volts AC, 50 Hz. The power outlets are equipped with the two-round-pin European standard plug. You might want a travel adaptor if your home country uses a different type of plug.

- **Emergency numbers**: In the event of an emergency, phone 112 to contact police, fire, or medical assistance.

- San Sebastian has decent internet connectivity, and a large number of hotels, eateries, cafes, and public spaces offer free Wi-Fi. For your mobile device, you might also think about getting a local SIM card or using the roaming services offered by your network operator.

- San Sebastian's public transit system, which includes cabs and buses, is effective. Additionally, the city is pedestrian and compact, making it simple to explore on foot. Consider buying a travel card or a multi-trip ticket if you frequently take public transit to save money and time.

- San Sebastian is regarded as a safe place for travellers in general. But it's always a good idea to practise basic safety measures. Watch out for pickpockets and keep a watch on your valuables, especially in crowded places. To cover any unanticipated incidents, travel insurance is also advised.

- San Sebastian is home to a number of tourist information centres where you can pick up maps, brochures, and help with any questions you might have. Near the city centre, on Boulevard Zumardia, is where you'll find the main tourism office.
- **Tipping**: While not required in San Sebastian, good service is appreciated. A service fee may be added to the bill at restaurants. If not, it is usual to leave a gratuity of 5–10%. Rounding up the tab or leaving loose change is customary at pubs and cafes.

Before your journey, don't forget to check for any unique travel limitations or prerequisites, such as visa requirements. Additionally, it's a good idea to purchase travel insurance to safeguard your assets while abroad.

Have a great trip, and take use of your time in San Sebastian!

Local Customs and Etiquette

To ensure a polite and pleasurable trip, it is good to become familiar with the regional customs and etiquette before visiting San Sebastian. Here are some crucial manners and traditions guidelines to remember:

- **Greetings**: A handshake is appropriate when meeting someone for the first time or in a formal situation. In less formal circumstances, friends or acquaintances may kiss each other on the cheeks.

- Spanish people, notably those in San Sebastian, have a reputation for being less strict about being on time. While it's ideal to arrive promptly for professional meetings or engagements, social events can begin a little beyond the scheduled hour.

- **Dining Etiquette:** It's polite to wait until the host or hostess invites you to sit down and begin eating when dining in restaurants or homes. Remember that Spanish mealtimes are frequently later than those in other countries, with lunch usually beginning at 1 or 2 PM and dinner at 9 or 10 PM.

- San Sebastian has a relaxed dress code, but it's still polite to be well-groomed whether dining out, visiting a place of worship, or going to a cultural event. Avoid exposing too much skin or wearing beachwear in public.

- Respect and decorum are highly regarded in Spanish society. When communicating with locals, using the words "por favor" (please) and "gracias" (thank you) is always appreciated. Greeting store owners and service personnel is also usual when entering and exiting establishments.

- **Tipping**: Although it is not required, San Sebastian appreciates tips for good service. It's customary to give a little tip in restaurants, typically between 5 and 10% of the total bill, unless a service charge is already included. Rounding up the tab or leaving loose change is usual at pubs and cafes.

- **Noise Levels:** Because Spanish people are more active and expressive in conversation, it's usual for public settings to be a little louder than you might be accustomed to. However, it's crucial to exercise consideration and refrain from speaking too loudly, especially in calmer settings.

- Smoking restrictions apply to all enclosed public areas, including bars, restaurants, and public transit. Be aware of the notice and rules since there are specified areas where smoking is permitted.

- **Respect for the Siesta**: Although it's less frequent to see in cities like San Sebastian, the siesta, or midday nap, the notion is still widely used in Spain. Although some people may still be sleeping in the afternoon, it is polite to be careful of noise levels at this time.

- San Sebastian is located in the Basque Country, and the Basques take great pleasure in their culture and sense of identity. Locals can appreciate an effort to demonstrate an interest in their way of life, for example by learning a few fundamental Basque phrases.

You'll foster positive interactions and have a more fulfilling experience in San Sebastian if you respect regional customs and adhere to proper etiquette. Take pleasure in getting to know the individuals you meet and experiencing the culture firsthand.

Safety Tips and Emergency Contacts

Prioritise your safety and be ready for any emergencies that might occur when visiting San Sebastian. Keep in mind the following safety advice and emergency numbers:

General Security

- Keep a watch on your valuables and be cautious of your surroundings, particularly in busy tourist locations.

- Never show off enormous sums of money or expensive objects in public.

- When out at night, stay in locations that are well-lit and populated.

- Be on the lookout for pickpockets and protect all of your possessions, including smartphones, purses, and wallets.

- Make sure the car is locked and that valuables are hidden when parked if you are renting a vehicle.

Numbers for emergencies

- Dial 112. This will connect you to emergency services such as police, fire, and medical care. The entire European Union may use this number.

- Alternatively, you can call the neighbourhood police department directly at (92). Health and Medical Services:

- There are numerous hospitals and medical facilities in San Sebastian that offer emergency medical care. Call 112 in the event of a medical emergency, or head straight to the closest hospital.

- It is advised to purchase travel insurance that offers aid in case of emergency and covers medical costs.

Travel Protection:

- Having complete travel insurance that covers unexpected medical costs, trip cancellations, and lost or stolen possessions is advised. Make sure you are familiar with the conditions of your insurance coverage.

Natural disasters and the weather:

- San Sebastian has a warm and temperate temperature, but it's always a good idea to check the forecast and be ready for alterations in the weather.

- Follow local authorities' instructions in the event of a natural catastrophe or extreme weather, and if necessary, take refuge in designated safe zones.

Local laws and ordinances

- Learn about the Basque Country and San Sebastian's local laws and regulations. Respect regional traditions, customs, and cultural nuances.

- Always keep proper identification on you, such as a passport that is still valid.

Services for Consuls:

- Before your trip, make a note of the embassy or consulate contact details in case you need consular help as a foreign traveller.

Always be aware of any advisories or notices concerning travel that may have been issued for the area you want to visit. For the most recent information and suggestions, contact the foreign affairs or state departments of your nation.

You may improve your safety and have a worry-free trip to San Sebastian by being alert, taking the required precautions, and being ready for eventualities.

Medical Facilities and Pharmacies

Both locals and visitors can find a variety of medical facilities and pharmacies in San Sebastian. You can use the following information to locate pharmacies and medical facilities in the city:

Medical Resources:

- The primary public hospital in San Sebastian, Hospital Universitario Donostia, provides a wide range of medical services and specialties. Paseo Dr. Beguiristain, s/n, San Sebastián, 20014.

- Private hospital offering comprehensive healthcare and specialist treatments is Hospital Quirónsalud Donostia. Address: 174 Paseo de Miramón, San Sebastián, 20014.

- A private medical facility that provides a range of medical specialisations and services is called Policlnica Guipzcoa. Address: 44 Calle Camino de Uba, San Sebastián, 20014.

- It's crucial to remember that in the event of a medical emergency, it is advised to call 112 or head straight to the emergency room of the closest hospital for prompt assistance.

- In San Sebastian, pharmacies are known as "Farmacias" and are widely dispersed around the city. They carry a sizable selection of prescription and OTC drugs. Some pharmacies also have bilingual employees who can help customers who speak English. The following San Sebastian pharmacies are listed:

- Farmacia Calle de Fermn Calbetón, 13, 20003 San Sebastian, Spain. Marta Elordui.

- Address for Farmacia Avenida y 16 Avenida de la Libertad, San Sebastián, 20004.

- Address for Farmacia Centro San Martin is 28 Calle de San Martin, San Sebastián, 20007, Spain.

While most pharmacies are open during regular business hours, there are others that are open 24/7 in case of an emergency. Consult with a pharmacist who can offer advice and recommendations if you need a specific drug or have any health-related worries.

It's always a good idea to check for the most recent information, including operation times and locations, before your visit because the information provided here is subject to change.

Transportation Options

San Sebastian offers a variety of transportation solutions to make the city and its surroundings easier. The following are some popular forms of transportation:

- **Public Buses:** The Dbus firm runs a sizable public bus network in San Sebastian. Buses are a practical and reasonably priced means of getting about the city and to nearby places. Most neighbourhoods and tourist destinations are covered by the bus routes. On the Dbus website or at bus stops, you may discover information about bus times, routes, and prices.

- **Taxis**: In the entire city, taxis are easily accessible. Taxis are available at designated taxi stands or can be hailed from the street. In San Sebastian, metre-based taxis may charge extra for carrying luggage or late-night trips. Since not all cabs take credit cards, it is essential to have sufficient cash on hand.

- **Trains**: San Sebastian has good rail connections to other Spanish and European cities. Estación del Norte, which is close to the city centre, serves as San Sebastian's primary train station. The trains are run by Renfe, whose website and train stations both allow ticket purchases and schedule checks.

- **Rental cars:** You may rent a car from a number of car rental companies in San Sebastian if you prefer the flexibility of having your own vehicle. You may explore the city and its surroundings at your own speed if you have a car. But bear in mind that finding parking in the city's core can be difficult, and certain places might have rules or need a parking permit.

- **Bicycles**: San Sebastian is a city that encourages cycling, and you may hire bikes there. For a few hours or a whole day, you can rent bicycles to tour the city's bike lanes and waterfront promenades. Rentals of shared bicycles through services like Donosti Bike are also possible.

- **Walking**: San Sebastian is a small, walkable city, making this a relaxing mode of transportation. Numerous attractions and the city's centre are conveniently walkable from one another. You can take in the scenery and find hidden treasures while walking.

- The city centre of San Sebastian features pedestrianised zones, which makes it more pleasant for people to walk there. Additionally, a lot of San Sebastian's sights, like La Concha Beach and the Old Town, are reachable on foot.

It's a good idea to verify schedules, prices, and any applicable restrictions or regulations before utilising any means of transportation.

You can select the mode of transportation that best meets your requirements while exploring San Sebastian by taking into account elements like convenience, price, and the location of your accommodations.

Language Guide and Useful Phrases

Knowing a few simple words and phrases can improve your interactions with locals and your overall experience in San Sebastian. Spanish is mainly used in San Sebastian, although Euskara, the Basque language, is also frequently spoken. Here is a language list with a few helpful words:

Greetings and Basic Phrases:
- Hello: Hola
- Good morning: Buenos días
- Good afternoon/evening: Buenas tardes
- Good night: Buenas noches
- Thank you: Gracias
- You're welcome: De nada
- Please: Por favor
- Excuse me: Perdón/Disculpa
- Yes: Sí
- No: No

Introductions:
- What is your name?: ¿Cómo te llamas?
- My name is...: Me llamo...
- Nice to meet you: Mucho gusto

Asking for Help:
- Can you help me, please?: ¿Puede ayudarme, por favor?
- Where is...?: ¿Dónde está...?
- I'm lost: Estoy perdido/a
- I need a doctor: Necesito un médico
- I don't understand: No entiendo

Ordering Food and Drinks:
- I would like...: Me gustaría...
- Can I see the menu, please?: ¿Puede darme el menú, por favor?
- A table for [number of people], please: Una mesa para [number of people], por favor
- Do you have vegetarian options?: ¿Tienen opciones vegetarianas?

- A glass of water, please: Un vaso de agua, por favor
- The bill, please: La cuenta, por favor

Getting Around:

- Where is the bus/train station?: ¿Dónde está la estación de autobuses/trenes?
- How much does a ticket cost?: ¿Cuánto cuesta un billete?
- Can you take me to [destination], please?: ¿Puede llevarme a [destination], por favor?
- Is it far from here?: ¿Está lejos de aquí?

Shopping:

- How much does it cost?: ¿Cuánto cuesta?
- Can I try this on?: ¿Puedo probárselo?
- Do you have a larger/smaller size?: ¿Tiene una talla más grande/más pequeña?

- I would like to buy this: Me gustaría comprar esto

Emergencies:
- Help!: ¡Ayuda!
- I need the police: Necesito la policía
- I need an ambulance: Necesito una ambulancia

Keep in mind that even just a few words in the language can make a big difference to the community. Don't be scared to give it a shot; if you need further help, many San Sebastian residents are also able to talk in English. Have fun while you're in San Sebastian!

CONCLUSION

In conclusion, San Sebastian is a dynamic and alluring location that provides a wide range of cultural experiences, scenic beauty, delectable cuisine, and thrilling activities.

San Sebastian has plenty to offer every traveller, whether they want to explore the quaint Old Town, soak up the sun on La Concha Beach, indulge in the world of Basque cuisine, or get involved in the regional customs and festivities.

You have learned a lot about San Sebastian from this thorough travel guide, including facts about its history, geography, modes of transportation, lodging options, must-see sights, outdoor activities, cultural experiences, shopping, and useful advice for having a safe and enjoyable trip. You'll be well-equipped to enjoy your time in this lovely city with this guide in hand.

Take time to enjoy the gorgeous environment that surrounds San Sebastian and don't forget to embrace the regional traditions, sample the delectable pintxos, interact with the welcoming residents, and try the local cuisine.

San Sebastian is likely to capture your heart and leave you with priceless memories, whether you're a foodie, nature enthusiast, history nerd, or just looking for a memorable vacation.

So gather your belongings, go out on your San Sebastian excursion, and acquaint yourself with the beauty and allure of this gem of the Basque Coast. Have fun on your voyage, and may it be full of joy, exploration, and amazing encounters!

Recap of San Sebastian Highlights

Explore the Old Town (Parte Vieja), the city's historic core, with its winding streets, quaint buildings, and lively atmosphere. Visit the neighbourhood bars to indulge in delectable pintxos (Basque tapas).

- **La Concha Beach**: Unwind on one of the most spectacular urban beaches in Europe, renowned for its beautiful crescent shape, crystal-clear waves, and charming promenade.

- Climb Monte Urgull for sweeping city views and to see the Castillo de la Mota, a former military stronghold. Don't overlook the famous Jesus Christ statue at the peak.

- Take the funicular up Monte Igueldo for stunning city views and revel in the old amusement park's vintage rides and attractions.

- Beachgoers and surfers alike will enjoy Zurriola Beach's fantastic waves and energetic environment. The Kursaal Congress Center and Auditorium are also located there.

- Walk along Paseo Nuevo for beautiful views of the sea, the Old Town, and the shoreline as it hugs the cliffs.

- **Miramar Palace**: Marvel at the opulence of this 19th-century palace set within lush grounds. It is an excellent place for a leisurely stroll and gives magnificent views of the bay.

- Discover the underwater world at the spectacular Aquarium Donostia, which is home to a broad range of aquatic life, including penguins, rays, and sharks.

- **Gastronomy**: Savour San Sebastian's culinary delights, which are renowned for their Michelin-starred eateries, authentic Basque cuisine, and pintxos culture. Don't pass up the opportunity to sample the regional cuisine.

- **Cultural Experiences**: Take part in regional celebrations, visit museums and art galleries, watch Basque pelota matches, and generally immerse yourself in the colourful culture and customs of the Basque country.

San Sebastian offers the ideal fusion of breathtaking natural scenery, fascinating history, delectable cuisine, and engaging cultural events. It's a place that genuinely offers something for everyone, making a trip there memorable and enjoyable.

Farewell From San Sebastian

From San Sebastian, goodbye! We sincerely hope you enjoyed discovering this magical city and taking advantage of everything it has to offer. San Sebastian leaves a lasting effect on those who visit, from the magnificent beaches and majestic surroundings to the delectable cuisine and active cultural scene.

Take with you the pleasure of experiencing the distinct ambiance of this coastal jewel, as well as the memory of the picturesque views, the flavour of the mouthwatering pintxos, and the warmth of the Basque hospitality.

Keep in mind that San Sebastian will always welcome you back anytime you choose to do so. Awaiting your return, may your journeys be chock-full of exciting new experiences and may the memories of your time in San Sebastian linger in your heart forever.

Goodbye and safe travels.

Printed in Great Britain
by Amazon

25251803R00155